THE
CALORIE
COUNTER

THE
CALORIE
COUNTER

A complete checklist of calories and carbohydrates

Patricia A. Judd, PhD, SRD
Gabi B. Reaidi, PhD

First published in Great Britain in 1981 by
Octopus Books Limited
59 Grosvenor Street
London W1

Second impression, 1982

© Hennerwood Publications Limited 1981

ISBN 0 86273 020 1

Made and printed in Great Britain by
Richard Clay (The Chaucer Press) Limited,
Bungay, Suffolk

Illustrations by Russell Barnett, Andrew Martin

CONTENTS

INTRODUCTION

STARTING OFF

If you are reading this book the chances are that you are worried about your weight; probably worried that you are too fat. If you are, you aren't alone – it has been estimated that half the people in this country are heavier than is good for them. That means you have a fifty-fifty chance of being overweight – but how do you tell?

Most people know if they have put on weight recently, clothes don't fit so well as they used to and an honest look in the mirror, without clothes, will often reveal the problem. A more objective view, though, is to compare your weight with tables showing the range of weight which is best for your height and sex.

First, though, you must be aware that it is really excess fat which is important, not weight itself. People may weigh heavily for other reasons. For example, athletes and others who develop large muscles can be above the ideal range of weight – but this is not fat. However, body weight is nearly always a good guide to body fat.

The most commonly used tables of weight for height were prepared by American insurance companies from the measurements of millions of their customers. Their statistics showed that people who were about 6 kg (12 lb) above the 'average' weight for their height had shorter lives. They therefore devised tables by calculating the weight at which fewest people were at risk from their evidence. They produced different tables for men and women and at each height there was a range of weights to allow for differences in frame size.

Unfortunately, there is no established way of measuring frame size. If you look at your hands and feet and compare them with other people's of the same height this may give you some idea. Similarly, looking at the width of shoulders and hips may help. However, the temptation is to assume that you have a large frame, then if you read your weight from the appropriate column in the tables you can kid yourself that you aren't fat. The charts on pages 8 and 9 are simplified versions of the ideal weight tables which remove this

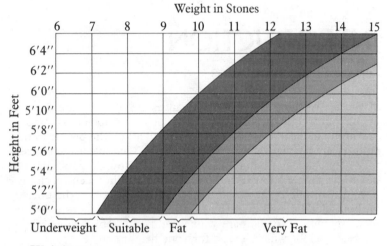

Weight Ranges – Men

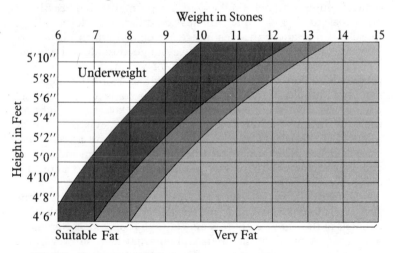

Weight Ranges – Women

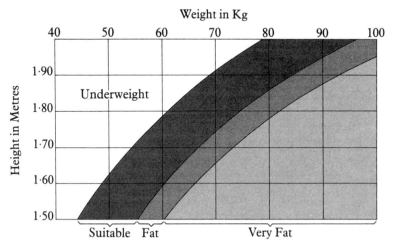

Weight Ranges – Men

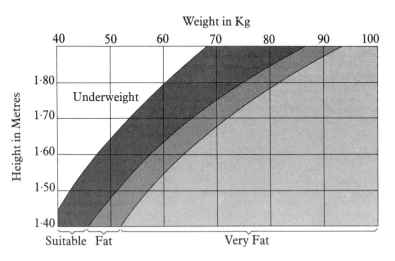

Weight Ranges – Women

temptation. They show a range of weights for each height – the 'suitable' weight range is based on the average ideal weight for the different frame sizes.

To use the charts
1. First measure your height, without shoes.
2. Weigh yourself, without shoes and preferably without clothes. If this isn't possible take off the heavy layers and then subtract 2–2.5 kg (4–6 lb) for the rest of your clothes.
3. Find the point on the chart where your height and weight intersect.

If your weight falls within the 'suitable' range you are probably alright. Health is only adversely affected if you are in the 'very fat' range but if your weight is in the 'fat' range you should not be too complacent. It may be relatively easy to reduce it now, whereas any increase will put you into the danger zone.

So if you've decided you are overweight – what can you do about it? It may help to understand why people put on weight in the first place and in order to do that you need to know a little about the way the body uses the food you eat.

THE ESSENTIAL NUTRIENTS

The food we eat has several functions. It is needed for growth in children, for repair of body tissues in adults and to provide the energy we need for all our activities. For these functions the main nutrients are the proteins, fats and carbohydrates. Mineral salts such as calcium, phosphates and others are needed for growth and maintenance of, for example, bones and teeth and some mineral salts are involved with the vitamins in ensuring the proper functioning of all the body's systems.

Through eating a variety of foods, we obtain a mixture of all these nutrients. The food is digested and broken down into simpler chemicals that the body can absorb and make use of.

Protein
In the body proteins are needed for construction and repair. All the tissues and organs in the body are made of protein: muscles, skin, heart and less obvious things such as nails and hair. During childhood the body needs a large amount of protein for growth and laying down of new tissues. In the adult the need is for replacement of worn out tissue only, so less protein is required.

In this country we eat far more protein than we need and the excess is used by the body to produce energy.

Since protein is the basis of all living tissue, all foods, whether vegetable or animal, contain some protein. The exceptions to this rule are foods which have been extracted from the original plant or animal. So, for example, sugar is a pure carbohydrate and vegetable oil or lard are pure fats. The table below gives an idea of some of the important sources of protein in the diet.

Food	Grams of Protein per 30 grams (1 oz)
Fish	3–7
Meat	5–7
Cheese	4–8
Milk	1
Pulse vegetables (dry)	5–8
Bread	2–3
Potatoes	0.4–1
Egg (1 only)	6

An adult needs to obtain 10% of his or her energy as protein each day. Therefore, on a 2000 Calorie diet, 200 Calories should be protein and, as protein supplies 4 Calories per gram, the total weight of protein intake per day will be 50 grams (1⅔ oz). From the table you can see that you could get all you need each day from half a pint of milk, 180 grams (6 oz) of meat or fish and four slices of bread.

Carbohydrates

These are the starches and sugars which make up about half of most people's diet. Their main function in the body is as an energy supply. Sugar is the most concentrated and purest carbohydrate and provides no other nutrients – it's just a source of energy. This applies to both brown and white sugar and for this reason these foods are said to contain 'empty calories', as are things like sweets and fizzy drinks. Sugars are also found in less concentrated form in all fruits.

Other carbohydrate-containing foods are cereals, e.g. breakfast cereals or flour, bread and pasta. Root vegetables, such as potatoes, also contain starch. The cereals and root vegetables contain other nutrients as well and are therefore useful items in the diet. Sometimes, however, the protein and other nutrients in foods such as flour are diluted by adding sugar and fat to make cakes and pastry. They then become largely sources of energy rather than important nutrients, which if not burnt up are converted to body fat.

Fats

The main sources of fat in the diet are butter, margarine, other cooking fats and oils and, less obviously, dairy products and meat. Even in very lean meat there is still a certain amount of hidden fat and similarly, oily fish like salmon or herring also have a high fat content. Other sources are cakes, biscuits and pastries.

In western countries we eat more fat than we need because fats make foods taste pleasant. In many foods the particular flavour we associate with that food is in the fat. We really only need to get about ten per cent of our energy from fat in order to satisfy the body's requirements. Most people eat much more than this.

Fats are a very concentrated energy source – for this reason anyone on a slimming diet should be careful to avoid too many high fat foods.

Mineral Salts

Several minerals are important for the healthy functioning of the body. These include sodium (as salt), potassium, magnesium, phosphate and others such as copper, iodine and zinc, which are only needed in very small amounts. If we eat a varied diet it is unlikely that we would go short of any of these.

Two minerals which are needed in larger amounts, and which can sometimes be low in the diet of people trying to slim, are:

Calcium

This is needed to build and maintain strong bones and teeth. Adults need about half a gram a day, children twice as much. This is usually obtained from milk, cheese and other dairy products in this country, although bread, to which calcium is added, is also a useful source. Other sources are canned fish, such as salmon and sardines, where the bones are eaten, and green vegetables.

Iron

This is needed for the red pigment in the blood, which carries oxygen to all the tissues. If there is insufficient iron in the diet, anaemia may result. This is not uncommon, especially in women, who lose iron in the menstrual blood loss.

Iron is found in meat (particularly offal such as liver and kidneys) and is easily absorbed from these animal foods. The iron in other foods is less well absorbed, so cereals and green vegetables may look good on paper but aren't so good in practice. Eggs used to be regarded as a good source of iron, but it's now recognized that the iron is poorly absorbed and may even lower the absorption of iron from other foods eaten with them.

Vitamins

There are thirteen different vitamins known to be important for a healthy body; they are chemically very different and without them the system cannot make use of the other essential nutrients. Some vitamins are associated with fat in foods and others with the non-fat part. These are called fat-soluble and water-soluble respectively. Fat-soluble vitamins are stored in the body and can be harmful in excess; surplus water-soluble vitamins are excreted, therefore are harmless.

Vitamin Fat-soluble	Function	Sources
A	Helps keep mucous membranes healthy. Essential for vision in dim light.	Dairy products; eggs; enriched margarine; cod liver oil. Also made from carotene in green plants and carrots.
D	Necessary for formation of healthy bones.	Cod liver oil; fatty fish e.g. herrings, kippers; dairy produce; enriched margarine. Also formed by the action of sunlight on skin.
E	Function not fully understood.	Cereals, especially wholemeal; eggs; butter; green leafy vegetables.
K	Essential for blood clotting.	Green leafy vegetables; fruits; nuts; wholegrain cereals.
Water-soluble		
B_1	Helps release energy from foods and makes best use of protein.	Wholegrain cereals; legumes; meat, especially pork and bacon, liver and kidney; yeast extract; flour.

Water-soluble	Function	Sources
B_2	As B_1	Milk; meat; liver; eggs; cheese; green leafy vegetables; yeast extract.
Nicotinic Acid	As B_1	Wholegrain cereals; pulses; meat, especially liver; fortified breakfast cereals.
Biotin	As B_1	Yeast; nuts; liver and kidney; green vegetables.
C	Important for healing and generally maintaining tissues.	Fruit, especially citrus; green vegetables; tomatoes; potatoes.
Folic Acid	For formation of all cells in the body, for blood formation.	Liver; pulses; wholegrain cereals; green vegetables.
B_6	General metabolism.	Meat; vegetables; yeast; wholegrain cereals.
B_{12}	Formation of new cells especially blood.	Meat, especially liver; dairy products. Absent from plants.
Pantothenic Acid	Used in metabolism	All foods.

Dietary fibre

Apart from the essential nutrients there is another constituent of food. Dietary fibre or roughage is the part of our food which can't be digested and therefore, although it is largely carbohydrate, it doesn't supply energy, i.e. it isn't included in the Calorie count.

Processing or refining foods often removes fibre and therefore the other nutrients in the food are concentrated and the energy value of the food is slightly higher. Apart from diluting the energy in foods, fibre may be useful to slimmers in other ways. Because foods with the fibre intact take more chewing, you may find that you eat less and because of its bulk fibre may help to make you feel full.

In the body fibre also increases the bulk and softness of the stools because it absorbs water as it passes through the digestive tract. It also speeds up the passage of stools through the system and if you have sufficient fibre in the diet you are unlikely to get constipated.

Foods which are high in fibre are bran or bran cereals and wholemeal bread is another good source. Pulse vegetables are high in fibre and fruit and vegetables are useful sources on a slimming diet, when you may be eating less cereals and potatoes.

A GOOD DIET

A good diet is one which supplies you with all the essential nutrients in the correct amounts. The best way to achieve this is to eat a varied diet. Include some of the high protein foods, e.g. two portions of either meat, fish, eggs or cheese each day. Have some cereal in the form of wholemeal bread or breakfast cereal and at least two portions of either cooked vegetables or salad. Have at least one portion of fruit each day and vary the type, the citrus fruits – oranges and grapefruit are highest in vitamin C. Avoid having too many high fat and sugary foods, even if you aren't trying to lose weight.

ENERGY BALANCE AND OVERWEIGHT

The fact that carbohydrate, fat and protein supply energy to the body has been mentioned several times – but what does this mean in terms of getting fat or staying slim?

The term ENERGY as used by scientists means 'the capacity to do work'. This applies equally to a machine or to the human body. The work may be carrying out some activity or just producing heat. In the body energy is used for all its functions, be it obvious ones like running upstairs or less visible like keeping the heart beating or maintaining breathing.

In order to provide energy the body needs a fuel of some sort and this is provided by the food we eat. In the same way as petrol is burnt in a car engine to keep it moving, the body burns food to supply energy for its activities. The energy in our foods is supplied mainly by carbohydrates and fats although proteins will be used if very little of the other nutrients is available or if protein makes up a high proportion of the diet.

The important thing to remember is that any energy put into the system must be used up through activities, visible or otherwise.

If more energy is obtained from food than is used up in activity then the excess is stored – as fat. On the other hand, if you use up more energy than you put in, the energy needed for activity will be drawn out of the store and you will lose weight.

Energy in equal to **Energy out**   Weight constant
Energy in more than Energy out   Gain weight
Energy in less than **Energy out**   Lose weight

MEASURING ENERGY

The energy used up in activity and that taken in as food is measured in kilocalories, more often just called Calories. Nowadays, under the more modern system, the terms kilojoule or Joule are also used. Both Joules and Calories are actually units of heat but Joules are much smaller than Calories.

1 Calorie = 4.2 Joules

Most people are still used to considering the energy value of food in Calories, so this term will be used throughout the book. Some foods, however, especially those made for slimmers already have the energy expressed in Joules on the packet. Joules can be converted to Calories by dividing them by 4.2.

The energy in food is supplied by carbohydrate, fat and protein. Protein and carbohydrate both supply the same number of calories, weight for weight. Fat is a much more concentrated source of Calories.

1 gram carbohydrate gives 4 kilocalories (Calories)
1 gram protein gives 4 kilocalories (Calories)
1 gram fat gives 9 kilocalories (Calories)

There is another source of energy which has not been mentioned yet – alcohol. Although it is not a carbohydrate it is used like one in the body.

1 gram of alcohol gives 8 kilocalories (Calories)

Looking at this in another way: if we ate an ounce (28.4 g) of pure protein, carbohydrate, fat or alcohol each would supply the following number of Calories:

1 ounce of protein gives 110 Calories
1 ounce of carbohydrate gives 110 Calories
1 ounce of fat gives 260 Calories
1 ounce of alcohol gives 200 Calories

In practice, though, few foods contain only one nutrient; most are mixtures of several. The energy provided by any food will therefore depend on the proportions of protein, fat and carbohydrate. Calorie values of foods can be calculated knowing the amounts of these constituents. For example, suppose a food contains 7 g of carbohydrate, 7 g of protein and 10 g of fat in 28.4 g (1 oz) – the rest may be made up of water. The protein and the carbohydrates supply 4 Calories per gram and the fat provides 9.

Therefore $7 \times 4 = 28$ carbohydrate Calories
$7 \times 4 = 28$ protein Calories
$10 \times 9 = 90$ fat Calories
Total Calories = 146 Calories per 28.4 g (1 oz) of the food

Different foods have different proportions of protein, carbohydrate and fat and therefore varying Calorie values.

Water has no Calorie content – so any food with a high water content will be low in energy. Dietary fibre also provides little, if **any** energy, so foods with a lot of water and fibre will be especially low in Calories, e.g. salad vegetables like celery or lettuce. On the other hand, fat is the highest source of energy, so foods such as butter, lard and oils should be avoided when possible.

WHY DO PEOPLE PUT ON WEIGHT?

In one way putting on weight is a normal part of life – from infancy until adult height and weight are attained you are gaining weight. At puberty also a certain amount of necessary fat is laid down. The problem is that some people, as well as using the energy for growth also gather a large store of fat.

This only applies to some people (though in this country it would seem to be about half the population) and we still don't really know the cause of obesity. Or perhaps we should say, we don't know why some people stay thin. One of the unsolved mysteries of nutritional science is why some people can eat large quantities of food without gaining weight, while others apparently eat less food and still get fat.

What can be said, however, is that if you are overweight you are taking or have taken at some time more energy than you needed to carry out the activities you were involved in.

This applies to any individual who is fat. However, as people's energy requirements vary so much, the level of food intake at which they gain weight also varies.

Two people of the same age, sex and height may have very different needs for energy – one may maintain weight on an intake of 1500 Calories a day, the other might lose weight slowly at the same level.

How can Calorie requirements be worked out?

Earlier, it was pointed out that all activity uses energy. The body's need for energy can be broken up into two parts. There is the RESTING energy – which is that needed just to keep all the body systems ticking over, i.e. to breathe, for the heart to beat, blood to circulate, digestion of food and so on. Anything else you do, from the moment you wake up in the morning, will need extra energy. This activity energy is sometimes called VOLUNTARY energy. To find your total energy requirement, you add the amount of voluntary energy needed to the resting energy. If you aren't a very active person, the resting energy will account for a large proportion of your energy needs. Resting energy requirements vary a lot from person to person, according to their metabolic rate. Metabolic rate is the rate at which the functions of the body proceed and varies according to age, sex and size. Typical values are around 1200 to 1400 Calories a day.

If you are a very active person who walks everywhere, runs upstairs and is constantly 'on the go' your resting energy will be proportionately less important. Very few people, however, use more voluntary energy than resting energy each day.

Different activities use up different amounts of energy – for example, sitting writing a letter uses very little, whereas the same amount of time spent digging the garden would use around five times as much. The chart on page 19, opposite shows the energy 'cost' of some activities. The absolute values don't really mean a lot as this varies according to body size, etc., but it gives an idea of the relative values.

You could calculate roughly how many Calories you use up in activities each day if you were prepared to keep a detailed record of all your activities during the day but you would still need to know your resting energy requirement – which is not so easy to measure – you would need a specially equipped laboratory.

So really we have to go back to the original 'energy balance' statement –

Approximate Energy Cost of Some Activities for a 70 kg Adult

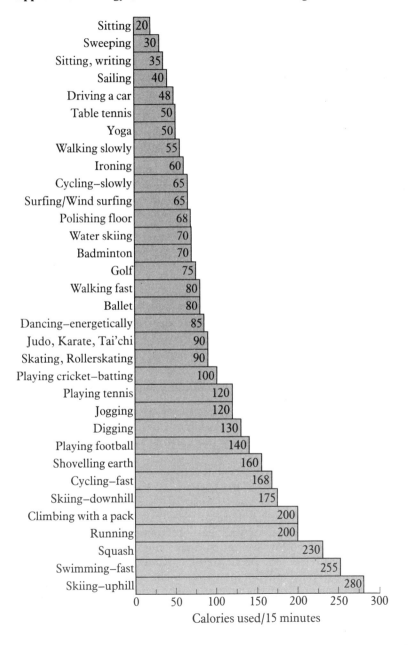

Activity	Calories used/15 minutes
Sitting	20
Sweeping	30
Sitting, writing	35
Sailing	40
Driving a car	48
Table tennis	50
Yoga	50
Walking slowly	55
Ironing	60
Cycling–slowly	65
Surfing/Wind surfing	65
Polishing floor	68
Water skiing	70
Badminton	70
Golf	75
Walking fast	80
Ballet	80
Dancing–energetically	85
Judo, Karate, Tai'chi	90
Skating, Rollerskating	90
Playing cricket–batting	100
Playing tennis	120
Jogging	120
Digging	130
Playing football	140
Shovelling earth	160
Cycling–fast	168
Skiing–downhill	175
Climbing with a pack	200
Running	200
Squash	230
Swimming–fast	255
Skiing–uphill	280

Calories used/15 minutes

If you are gaining weight you are taking in more energy than your body needs.

There are two ways this could have happened:
1. If you have been taking in more energy in your food than you have been using up.
2. If you have been eating the same amount as you were when your weight was lower, but becoming less active.

There seem to be several danger points at which people gain weight – many people say they started to gain weight when they got married; for some women pregnancy is the time when they gain weight and they don't lose it after their babies are born. Gaining weight because of using less energy is common in people who are getting older – the so-called middle-aged spread. This doesn't necessarily happen as you get older, though there is some evidence that the metabolic rate slows down a little with age and this will tend to make weight gain more likely. Any change in lifestyle which means cutting down on the amount of exercise you do may let the weight creep on. Perhaps active sports may give way to being just a spectator. Illness may also restrict activity and being overweight itself may slow down movement. It's a lot more effort to play tennis if you are carrying an extra stone of weight and you may be less likely to go swimming if you feel you look unattractive in a bathing costume.

Exercise is a useful way of keeping off the weight. You only need to take in 100 extra Calories a day over a period of months to gain weight. The daily walk to work, even if it's only for ten minutes, may be the thing which stops you getting fatter and once you stop . . .

HOW CAN YOU TAKE OFF WEIGHT?

It must be obvious that in order to lose weight you have to take in less energy than you need for your level of activity, so that you will use up the store of fat to produce energy and will gradually get thinner. It may seem that there are two ways of doing this – either by cutting down on food or by increasing the amount of energy you use up. So – can you lose weight by increasing your level of exercise?

Logically this should be so – in practice you have to increase activity by a large amount in order to make much difference to your weight. For example, the average person would have to walk about 160 kilometres (100 miles) to lose just over 1 kg (2 lb) of fat. For this reason few people find that increasing exercise alone will take off weight as fast as they want to lose it. However, if you decided to do more exercise regularly, such as walking to work or the shops instead of driving, you would probably lose some weight over the course of months, provided you didn't eat more because the extra exercise increased your appetite.

Exercise may have other benefits in a slimming regime though. It helps tone your muscles and may make you less flabby as you lose weight. A brisk walk or a long swim also often gives you a feeling of wellbeing, irrespective of the 'good' it is doing and may help take your mind off food while you're dieting.

What sort of exercise?

In order to be of any benefit the exercise should be done regularly and often – walking or cycling for 30 minutes a day is more useful than playing squash once a week, even though the latter may leave you feeling exhausted. Some experts maintain that 'regular' is the most important word – and that regular exercise increases the metabolic rate generally, even when you are sleeping. Jogging is a popular form of exercise and seems to help prevent heart attacks even if it doesn't take off weight. Other ways of taking exercise include walking, cycling or dancing or you could take up (or resume) a sport, such as tennis or swimming. Or you may prefer to carry out a programme of exercise at home each day.

Whichever type of exercise you choose it should be regular and reasonably active – i.e. use up more energy than just sitting. One warning though, if you haven't been very active for some years, particularly if you are over 35, very overweight or have a history of high blood pressure or heart disease or back or knee problems – you should check with your doctor before exercising vigorously.

So, exercise may help in a weight reduction programme but if you want to lose weight at a reasonable rate there is no alternative to cutting down on energy intake. This need not mean eating less food – some foods contain very little energy and can be eaten freely. What is essential is that while reducing your Calorie intake you still eat a balanced diet, with sufficient protein, minerals and vitamins. The way to do this is to have as 'normal' and as varied a diet as possible.

WHICH DIET?

The aim is to find a diet which suits the life you lead and is relatively easy to keep to, so that you develop a new pattern of eating, which becomes permanent. Then you'll be less likely to put the weight back on again.

Example of food record sheet

Day	Time	Place	Who with	Food eaten
Monday	8.30	Home	Alone	Coffee + boiled egg
	11.00	Work	Colleagues	Coffee + biscuit
	1.30	Work	Colleagues	Cheese sandwich + yogurt
	3.00	Work	Colleagues	Tea
	7.30	Home	Family	Grilled pork chop + salad + potatoes + apple

Calorie value	Hungry	Mood	Activity
30 + 80	no	sleepy	getting ready for work
30 + 60	no	busy	working at desk
530 + 75	yes	normal	reading newspaper
30	no	busy	working at desk
565 + 100 + 100 + 60	no	relaxed	sitting at table
1660			

There are many types of diet available. Two of the most popular are the Calorie Controlled method and the Low Carbohydrate diet described here. Counting Calories is the basic method and many of the other diets around are just ways of taking the effort out of this by giving specific menus or meals, which are designed with low Calorie foods. Carbohydrate counting is a refinement of Calorie counting, which works by cutting down Calories in two ways: directly by reducing carbohydrate-containing foods and indirectly by lowering fat intake.

One way you can help yourself to decide which diet is suitable is to keep a record of everything you eat for a few days. An example of such a record is given on the previous pages. Write down not only what you eat but when, where and why. By doing this you may get some insight into the reasons you eat, apart from real hunger. Then you can see what changes, if any, are needed in your life to help cope with being on a diet. A daily record will also reveal whether you normally eat a lot or a little and help you to decide on the level of Calories or carbohydrates you should eat. Once you have decided on the diet there's no real benefit in keeping constant records like this, they may even substitute for the real business of keeping to the diet you have chosen.

The descriptions below may help you to decide which is the most useful diet for you.

WHICH DIET SUITS YOU?

The Calorie Controlled plan is useful:
(a) if you have only a little weight to lose.
(b) if you don't mind weighing and measuring foods and keeping a running total of the Calories you've eaten.
(c) if you find it difficult to resist sweet and starchy foods.
(d) if you tend to nibble between meals.
(e) if you've already lost some weight by another method but seem to be stuck.

The Low Carbohydrate diet is useful:
(a) if you are prepared to do some weighing and measuring but not to devote a lot of effort to this.
(b) if you have a family to cook for or eat out often with friends or in restaurants.
(c) if you have a lot of weight to lose or you have never tried to diet before.
(d) if you feel you can cut out sweet and starchy foods and alcohol without feeling deprived.
(e) if you are not tempted to nibble.

THE CALORIE CONTROLLED METHOD

Basically this involves setting a limit on the number of Calories you take each day and counting the Calories in the foods you choose to eat.

So first you must decide on your Calorie intake. This can be done by working out your energy requirements and cutting your intake below this level. It can also be done by working out the Calorie content of what you are eating at the moment and cutting down on that. In practice the Calorie level chosen is usually between 1000 and 1500 Calories per day.

1500 Calories are suitable if:

(a) you are physically very active, so your energy needs are high (e.g. an athlete, or a mother with active young children).

(b) you are used to eating large meals and would find it difficult to keep to 1000 Calories.

(c) you have more than 12 kg (2 stones) to lose. It is better to start with a higher limit as you will have to keep to the diet for a long time in order to reach your goal and this will be easier at a higher Calorie level.

1000 Calories are suitable if:

(a) you don't eat much at the moment.

(b) you are not very active (e.g. a desk worker).

(c) you have less than 12 kg (2 stones) to lose.

The lower Calorie limit is also useful for people who have already lost some weight but whose weight loss has slowed down or stopped. As long as you are eating fewer Calories than you are using up you will lose weight. The important thing is to choose a level which you can keep to. If you set it too low it's unlikely you'd be able to keep to it long enough for it to be effective.

The level can be set at 1200, 1400 or whatever suits you, but it is not advisable to go below 1000 Calories without medical supervision. Of course that doesn't mean you can't go below that level occasionally, you may find that you want to save some Calories for a special meal or celebration, then you might take 800 Calories for a couple of days to make up for an extra 400 that day. Similarly, your Calorie intake may be unevenly spread over the week; 5 days of 1200 and 2 of 2250 is the same as 1500 Calories a day and the weight loss will be comparable but the irregular count may suit a lifestyle where weekends involve 'social' eating.

How to manage the diet

Remember, it is important to maintain a nutritionly healthy diet. You would lose weight if you took all your 1000 Calories as chocolate cake or cream buns, but this wouldn't be good for your health.

The ideal then is to select a sensible variety of foods within the Calorie limit you set yourself. A good general rule is to keep about half your Calorie allowance for foods which are high in essential nutrients, such as meat, fish, eggs, green vegetables and fruit. In practice this means avoiding high fat foods as these have most Calories and to some extent avoiding high carbohydrate foods.

To start with, it is useful to weigh foods in order to calculate the Calorie value of your meals with reasonable accuracy – it is very difficult to estimate the weight of portions when you aren't used to it. After a while you will get used to the size of portions and it will be enough just to check occasionally to ensure you aren't under-estimating the size, especially if you stop losing weight.

It may seem, to start with, that you spend all your time looking up Calorie values and doing arithmetic. The Calorie values of foods you eat often will soon become second nature though and you won't find it such a chore.

THE LOW CARBOHYDRATE DIET

This diet, devised by Professor John Yudkin, relies on cutting sugary and starchy foods to a minimum. It is therefore slightly simpler than the Calorie counting method: you only need to know which foods contain carbohydrate and how much, rather than having to add up the Calorie values of all the items in your diet. Cutting out carbohydrates, especially foods that contain no other nutrients, like sugar and sweets, is obviously going to reduce your Calorie intake. Indirectly, carbohydrate counting will also cut down your fat intake: it's difficult to eat butter without bread to put it on and cakes and pastries, which are high in fat, will be omitted because of their carbohydrate content.

How to go about it

The carbohydrates in food are expressed in grams or units. One unit is equal to 5 grams of carbohydrate and the tables at the back of the book give values in units to make the arithmetic simpler.

To lose weight you need to limit yourself to between 10–16 units (50–80 grams) per day. In practice this means cutting out all sugary, sweet foods and restricting the amount of starchy foods you eat. Alcohol must also be avoided; although this is strictly not a carbohydrate, it is used like one by your body.

The diet allows you to eat as much as you like of other foods, so you needn't feel deprived or hungry, BUT a word of warning is necessary. If you find you aren't losing weight as quickly as you expected – even though you are within your carbohydrate allowance – you should do a quick check on your Calorie intake. It is possible to eat a low carbohydrate diet and still exceed your Calorie needs. This is because some foods, though they contain no carbohydrates still supply energy in the form of protein and fat; so, if you eat large quantities of these you won't lose weight. Foods, such as cheese or meat, are easy to eat in relatively large amounts and cream is another high fat food to beware of.

Planning your diet – general points
Once the diet is chosen, you need a strategy for maintaining it, for example, you should work out a meal pattern which suits you. Research has shown that many people lose weight more quickly if they eat small frequent meals, rather than one or two large ones each day. Eating little and often seems to speed up the metabolic rate. This is not always possible; a compromise is to have three meals each day, with small snacks in between. Eating a little breakfast and lunch and then having one huge meal in the evening is probably bad for several reasons:

- you may be very hungry and take in more energy than you would in 3 small meals;
- if you eat several meals, spread over the day, you'll probably use up more energy in activity between meals than if you eat a large meal in the evening and slump down in front of the television;
- a large late meal stops some people sleeping and increases the possibility of a midnight picnic;
- you also use a small amount of energy at each meal to digest and absorb your food and this is likely to be greater throughout the day if you eat three or four small meals than if you eat a single large one.

People sometimes try to lose weight by skipping a meal – this isn't a good idea either. If you are used to eating three meals a day and then miss out one you are bound to get hungry and be tempted to eat, usually something with as many Calories, but not as good nutritionally as the meal you missed.

This applies especially to breakfast – often regarded as 'the most important meal of the day'. Certainly people who are used to eating breakfast may suffer if they miss it out. They may tend to feel hungry and irritable by the middle of the morning and want to eat.

However, if you can't cope with breakfast in the early morning, it is better to plan to eat something later on than to force yourself.

How much food you eat at each meal is up to you. If you are used to large meals then you can continue these, but will have to be selective about what makes up the meal. Choose low Calorie foods to make up the bulk of the meal (see table 2), large portions of vegetables and an extra salad. Or start the meal with a portion of soup: a consommé or a home-made vegetable soup, to fill you up.

Plan your diet so you don't feel hungry – save some of your allowance for the evening if you know you always feel hungry while you are watching the television.

Remember you are trying to find a way of eating which suits your way of life and at the same time enables you to lose weight.

HOW CAN YOU START SLIMMING?

It's all very well to theorize about diets and exercise programmes – some people manage this but get no further, so how can you get started and continue successfully?

Motivation
Firstly you have to want to be slimmer – for whatever reason – be it that you want to look better or for health reasons. It's no use if someone else wants you to lose weight (unless it's your doctor), the motivation must come from you.

It may help to list all the reasons why you want to lose weight and then put them in a positive way. For instance 'I look awful in trousers' is a reason for wanting not to be fat; 'I'll wear size 12 jeans and look good' is an incentive to lose weight. Similarly 'I feel heavy and tired' and 'I'll soon be able to walk to work without feeling tired' are negative and positive sides of the same idea. Most people can find several positive reasons for wanting to get thinner and use these as incentives when the willpower is flagging.

Setting targets
One target you need to decide on is how much you want to lose. This can be worked out with the charts at the beginning of the book. If you have a lot of weight to lose, e.g. if your weight falls in the 'very fat' section of the graph, it's better to set yourself intermediate targets. For example, plan to lose the first six kilograms (the first stone) in a month or five weeks and then have a month when you aim to relax the diet and just maintain weight. Then start again and allow yourself six or seven weeks to lose the next 6 kg (1 stone). Also you should consult your doctor to check how much weight you should lose.

A few notes on weighing yourself may be appropriate here:

(a) Weigh yourself once a week, on the same scales. If you step on the scales every other day, you may be discouraged to find you've lost nothing though you have been trying hard. On the other hand you may find you haven't gained anything when you've cheated and be tempted to do it more often.

(b) Weigh yourself at the same time of day. You can be as much as a kilogram (2 lb) heavier in the evening than in the morning. Wear the same clothes each time, or preferably no clothes at all.

(c) Don't cheat – stand squarely on the scales – if you move around on bathroom scales you can often change the reading.

How much can you expect to lose?

You have to be realistic about what weight loss you accept each week. The actual loss will depend on the difference between your energy requirement and your intake. That is – if you need 2500 Calories to maintain weight and eat 1250, you are short of about 1250 Calories and will lose weight. If you eat 1750 Calories, you will probably still lose weight but more slowly. So to some extent you can control the rate at which you get thinner. With a Calorie deficit of 1000 Calories a day most people can expect to lose 0.5–1.0 kg (1–2 lb) per week.

Sometimes the weight lost in the first week is much more than this, up to 2, $2\frac{1}{2}$ or even 3 kg (5, 6 or 7 lb), depending on your initial weight. This is because at the beginning of a diet the body gets rid of its carbohydrate store and the water stored with it. This is seen on any diet, but is often more pronounced on the low-carbohydrate diet. It is very encouraging, but it isn't fat which is lost and you can't expect the weight loss to continue at this rate.

You may find that you lose $1–1\frac{1}{2}$ kg (2–3 lb) in the first weeks, but the rate of loss slows down slightly after a while. If you have a lot of fat to lose you may find that after you have lost a stone or two you stop losing any at all. This may be the time to switch to a low Calorie diet if you have been following the low carbohydrate regime or to lower your daily Calorie allowance if you are already counting Calories. This is where it pays to have settled for a slightly higher Calorie intake to start with. As you get slimmer, unfortunately, you may find that your Calorie requirement seems to fall and you may have to cut down more to maintain the same rate of weight loss. One of the reasons for this is that as you get slimmer, you actually need less energy to move around. Resting energy is also related to body size and is lower the smaller you are. People who have slimmed and then regained weight often notice this most. Their bodies seem to adapt very quickly when they reduce their energy intake and they have to eat even less than before to achieve the same weight loss.

There is no point in expecting to lose a large amount in a couple of months, far better to lose it slowly and reeducate yourself to a sensible way of eating, which will enable you to stay slim.

Another point to remember is that different people have different energy needs, so if you are comparing your weight loss with that of a friend, don't be discouraged if theirs is faster. As long as you are losing weight the diet is working.

There may be times when your weekly weight loss is less than you expected. This may be because you have eaten more than you thought you had, or, for women, because of water retention before a period. You can't use this as an excuse two weeks running though, as the water will be lost afterwards. There will be weeks when weight loss is slow but you should aim to keep losing slowly.

Carrying on

Once you've begun it takes a lot of willpower to keep going. It also takes patience. Remember it takes a long time to lose weight, if you ate nothing at all you would only lose about 360 g (12 oz) a day or $2\frac{1}{2}$ kg ($5\frac{1}{4}$ lb) in a week and you couldn't keep that up for long.

Losing weight is not easy and the most you can do is to reduce the difficulties as much as possible. If you kept a chart of food habits as suggested earlier you will probably have worked out the times during the day when you'll be tempted to eat.

Friends and family are not always helpful. If you have the sort of friends who say they 'like you best as you are' and offer you your favourite foods as soon as they know you're on a diet – don't tell them. On the other hand, it sometimes helps if you tell people, they may encourage you to keep at it. Some of the problems people find when they are trying to lose weight are outlined in the following pages.

MAINTAINING WEIGHT

Once you have reached your target don't be tempted to go back to your old eating habits. You now have to find the level at which you can maintain weight. This may sound easy after all the effort that's gone into getting slim but it's not so easy – many people put back on the weight that they've lost so painstakingly – and in much less time than it took to lose it. One of the problems is that the body adjusts to a lower energy intake. There is evidence to show that the metabolic rate slows down and as this is a major factor in your energy requirement you need fewer Calories to maintain weight. Also as you are slimmer your activities don't use so much energy; there is less of you to carry around.

So, suppose you have lost weight by Calorie counting. You used to maintain weight on 2000 Calories a day and lost weight on 1000 Calories. You now have to find your new level. The best way is to carry on weighing yourself once a week and gradually increase your intake. Try 1200 Calories the first week and then 1400 until you find the level at which you gain weight. Then go back one or two steps and stay at that level.

If you've been losing weight using the low-carbohydrate method, you can increase your energy intake by either of two ways (or a mixture of both). You may have got used to doing without sugary and starchy foods and may find it easier to do without them completely rather than have a small amount. In that case you could increase your intake of carbohydrate free foods like meat or cheese.

Alternatively, you might want to have more bread and potatoes – in that case increase your carbohydrate units e.g. from 10 to 15 or from 16 to 20. It's best not to do it all at once though as the body will store the excess carbohydrate along with some water and your weight may shoot up rapidly.

Apart from that the same rules apply as with Calorie counting – you must find a level at which your weight is steady. Don't let the weight go up by more than 1 or 2 kg (2–4 lb). If you find this is happening, go back to a strict diet until you get it under control.

COMMON PROBLEMS

Hunger

Very often people complain of being hungry when they start a diet. Sometimes this is really because they aren't eating enough. The solution is to make sure you have enough of the bulky low energy foods at mealtimes and allow extras for the times when you know you get hungry. It helps to have large portions of vegetables at meal times and in between a cup of tea or coffee may sometimes suffice. Very often just the thought of being on a diet makes people think about food much more. If they weren't dieting they probably wouldn't consider having a biscuit with their coffee – the fact that they 'can't' have it makes them envy the thin friend who seems to be constantly tucking in.

Sometimes you may find that you are always hungry at a certain time of day. A common problem is evening eating. You may find that you manage very well all day but come the evening you can't keep away from the fridge. This is often not real hunger but stems from boredom or stress. The evening is a time when all the problems of the day come to the fore and you may turn to food for 'comfort'. One solution is to arrange your diet so that you have some food left to eat in the evening. Another is to try to find out why you want to eat and then deal with the cause or find some way of taking your mind off eating. Perhaps this is the time to go swimming or take the dog for a walk – not to the nearest pub!

Dieting is boring

Thinking about what you eat all the time can certainly lead to boredom. The diet itself need not be boring though. Make sure you have a varied diet – make use of all the range of fruits and vegetables that is available nowadays. Try new fruits you haven't eaten before and give yourself treats – have a piece of fresh pineapple instead of an apple now and then or eat something you wouldn't normally have. There are many low Calorie recipe books available now and it is not too difficult to find recipes which exclude flour or other carbohydrate foods. Even if you are cooking for a family there is no reason why they shouldn't eat the same food, they can fill up on potatoes and bread. Low Calorie recipes tend to be low fat and this is healthier for the whole family.

Make eating an occasion – set the table and make your meal look attractive, especially if you are eating alone. Don't read or watch TV while you are eating – concentrate on the food.

Allow yourself an occasional treat. If you crave chocolate there's no reason why you shouldn't include a small bar of your favourite kind in your Calorie allowance once or twice a week. This will need rather more manipulation on a low carbohydrate diet as chocolate contains a lot of carbohydrate. However, if you chose this diet, chocolate is probably not one of your problem foods.

Keeping to a diet is difficult on special occasions

This is true. It's unlikely that the caterers at a wedding or a special meal will make allowances for slimmers – even though there are so many of them these days!

The solution to this is to plan ahead or compensate afterwards. The former is better as after the event the good intentions may fade away. If you know you are going to be eating a special meal, the best idea is to cut down on your energy intake for a couple of days before. Say you are going to a wedding and your normal Calorie intake is 1250 per day. You could cut down to 1000 for two days before and this will give you 500 Calories to play with on the day. If you are counting carbohydrates it is often easier to manage special meals just by avoiding the carbohydrate-containing foods.

The same system can be used at Christmas, when it is often very difficult to keep to a diet, and when people around you will often do their best to dissuade you from it anyway. Cut down for two or three days before the holiday, then you can eat the Christmas pudding, mince pies and other special foods. If you don't manage to do any of this don't regard it as the end of the world, or the end of the diet – just get back on to it as soon as you can.

Eating out can be a problem

You can cope with the occasional restaurant meal in the same way as special occasion meals – plan ahead. If you often eat out or you are asked out unexpectedly, then you should try to choose the least 'harmful' foods. This isn't always easy, but it is usually possible to find some items on the menu which are suitable (see table 3).

The low carbohydrate diet is often easier to manage in restaurants – and so is probably the best diet for those people who regularly eat out. It's relatively easy to leave the bread, avoid potatoes and have an extra vegetable; choose a little cheese instead of pudding. In fact the Calorie counting dieter can follow the same sort of pattern as well as avoiding dishes with sauces as these are usually high in fat and hence Calories. Obvious fat can also be cut off. Many dishes in restaurants will be high in fat, so it's best to stick to plain items and have fruit or cheese for dessert.

Other useful hints are:

Eat slowly, take small portions on your fork. Put your cutlery down between mouthfuls and chew the food well.

Drink slowly – if your glass is empty it's likely to be refilled. Have a glass of water as well as wine and drink this more often.

Refuse to let well-meaning friends or waiters give you second helpings.

Remember – you don't have to eat everything on the plate!

What about drinking?

It depends what you mean by drink. Contrary to some peoples' belief water is not fattening. Restricting intake will not make you lose weight faster. So you can drink as much water as you like. This includes black tea and coffee, calorie-free minerals and fizzy drinks, which are little else but water. If you put milk in the drink then you must take account of this and if you like sweetened drinks an artificial sweetener may be useful. If you are the sort of person who constantly drinks tea or coffee throughout the day you may find the new 'light' milks or skimmed milk useful. Light milk has about three-quarters of the Calorie content of whole milk and skimmed milk has half.

The real problem, though, may be alcoholic drinks – and arises in a pub or on other social occasions. Alcohol produces 8 Calories per gram and some drinks, like beer, also contain quite a lot of carbohydrate. The carbohydrate units and Calories can add up rapidly in a few hours in a pub. Again the solution is to plan ahead if you can and save some of your allowance for drinks at a party or special occasion. Don't do it too often as alcoholic drinks rarely supply anything else except Calories and a feeling of wellbeing which may make you much less careful about what you're eating.

It is possible to substitute other drinks for alcoholic ones. There are many low Calorie 'mixers' like tonic water or soda available now as well as low Calorie soft drinks. These are usually low in carbohydrate as well. No one needs to know that you haven't got gin with your tonic, or whisky with your ginger ale. If slimline drinks aren't available, choose tomato juice or other unsweetened fruit juices.

Otherwise, make yourself familiar with the Calorie and carbo-hydrate values of drinks and choose the lowest – for example a tot of gin with a low Calorie mixer is better than a pint of beer.

When you are at a party or in a pub remember that the 'bits and pieces' passed round with the drinks are usually also high in energy. A packet of crisps has about 150 Calories and a small packet of peanuts nearly 200. It's easy to consume half your day's intake without noticing.

PREPARING AND COOKING YOUR FOOD

When you are counting Calories or carbohydrates you should aim to cook foods in ways which retain as much of the food value as possible, yet avoid adding extra Calories.

If you are following the low carbohydrate regime, you ob-viously do not want to use sugar and flour in cooking. If you are using the Calorie counting method, you will want to avoid adding fat as well. If possible, it's also a good idea to get rid of some of the fat contained in certain foods, particularly meat. Some hints on choosing, preparing and cooking various foods are given below.

Vegetables
These are the mainstay of any slimming diet; they can usually be eaten freely to add bulk to the diet (except for starchy root vegetables like potatoes and beetroot). They are also important as they provide several of the essential vitamins and are a source of dietary fibre.

In order to retain the maximum amount of vitamin C, prepare fresh vegetables as near to cooking time as possible and cook them only for the length of time necessary to make them palatable. This means that they are still crisp when you eat them. Don't keep them warm after cooking either, as the vitamins are lost quickly then. Frozen vegetables are just as good as fresh ones, especially if the 'fresh' are not very fresh, vitamin C particularly is lost on storage.

To keep Calories down, the best ways of cooking are steaming, boiling or baking. Don't fry, as this will increase the Calorie value several fold. This is especially true of things like onions, mushrooms and potatoes which absorb a lot of fat in cooking. Don't be tempted to serve them with butter either, use chopped herbs to make them look attractive and add flavour.

Salads are obviously very useful, but don't be tempted to add mayonnaise or salad cream, which are both full of fat. There are low fat dressings available now or you can try just using either vinegar, lemon juice, yogurt or cottage cheese as the basis of your own dressing.

Vegetables are also useful for making low Calorie soups. They can be cooked in any number of combinations and used as the first course of a meal or as a meal on their own with a little grated cheese and wholemeal bread.

Meat and fish
When buying meat choose lean cuts. These need not be the most expensive, stewing steak is just as lean as fillet, once the visible fat has been removed, it just needs a longer cooking time. Some varieties of meats have less fat than others; choose the low fat ones more often. The fat content and hence the Calories increase in the following order, assuming you remove all the visible fat and don't eat the skin on poultry: chicken, turkey and offal; pork; beef; lamb; duck and goose.

Try to avoid meat products like beefburgers and sausages, which have bread or cereal added as well as being high in fat.

When you buy fish avoid fatty varieties such as herring or kippers and choose white fish e.g. cod, haddock and plaice, which have fewer calories. If you are buying frozen fish select fillets or steaks without batter or breadcrumbs added. If you are using canned fish, e.g. tuna, drain off as much oil as possible.

There are three watchpoints to observe when cooking meat or fish. Firstly, remove all visible fat from meat before cooking. Secondly, choose a method which will reduce the fat within the food. For example, by grilling steak, chops or bacon some of the fat will drain off and if you heat minced meat gently in a saucepan some of the fat will run out and can be poured off. Thirdly, try not to add any cooking fat. There is no need to fry vegetables for stews or casseroles; just put all the ingredients together with some well-flavoured stock and cook. If, however, you want to 'seal' meat before cooking it in a casserole or stew, use a non-stick pan and a quick spray of one of the new spray-on oils.

Fish sometimes needs a little fat if it is grilled or baked, if necessary brush on a very little melted butter or oil.

Another way of cooking low fat meats or fish is to bake them in foil together with vegetables for flavour. You can also use roasting bags or foil to roast meat and pour off fat before serving. If you want to make gravy, cool the juices and skim off the fat. Another way of removing fat from stews, etc., is to dip ice cubes into them. The fat will solidify on the ice and can be taken off.

Dairy products

Choose skimmed milk whenever possible, as it still has all the protein, but only half the Calories of ordinary milk. You can use it to make relatively low Calorie sauces using cornflour rather than fat and flour. If you are using ordinary milk let the cream rise to the surface, then skim it off. Don't buy homogenized milk as the cream won't separate.

Cheeses such as cottage or curd cheese have fewer Calories than cream cheese or hard cheese; if you like a hard cheese the lowest fat one is Edam.

Fruit and puddings

Fresh fruit is the obvious choice for dessert; avoid canned fruit in syrup and the concentrated sugars in dried fruit. If you stew fruit don't add sugar, add an artificial sweetener if you want a sweet taste. Remember that if you use saccharin you should add it after cooking to avoid the bitter taste. If you want a more substantial sweet course, add custard made with skimmed milk, cornflour and artificial sweetener or add plain yogurt. This is also delicious with chopped fruit and is lower in energy than proprietary fruit yogurts, as these have added sugar.

Other types of puddings make use of gelatine e.g. jelly made with fruit juice and fruit. Adding whisked egg white will enable you to increase the bulk of these kinds of desserts without increasing Calories very much, e.g. as an ingredient in mousses or whips.

If a particular recipe calls for cream – go one step down the scale, for example instead of double cream use single, instead of single use milk or yogurt. Obviously, cakes and pastry should be omitted wherever possible because of their fat content.

Using the Tables:

The values given in the three following tables cannot be regarded as absolute values for any food item you eat. The only way to find the real value of all food would be to chemically analyse it. However, they are accurate enough for you to control your Calorie or carbohydrate intake.

The calculations for the tables have been worked out using ounces as the standard measure. However for those who think metric the equivalents have been given in brackets. They are exact conversions (1 oz × 28.4 g) rounded up to whole grams, except that the 1 oz portions have been rounded up to 30 g for convenience. As kitchen scales are not so accurate when you are measuring you will find it easier to round up or down to the nearest 5 grams so if for example you are weighing 57 g of cooked dahl, 55 g is the amount to aim for; whereas with 114 g of roast forerib you would measure 115 g.

No distinction has been made for fluid ounces, they are treated the same as ounces.

TABLE 1

The Calories and carbohydrate units are given per oz (30 grams) and per portion. The portion size is described in the final column. In some cases the portion size is left as 1 oz (30 g), e.g. for raw weights when the food would be weighed before cooking.

All Calorie values have been rounded up or down to the nearest 5 Calories, thus some of the figures given for the portions are not direct multiples of those given for 1 oz (30 g). The exception is values below 5 Calories per oz where the nearest whole number is given.

Carbohydrate units are expressed to the nearest $\frac{1}{4}$ of a 5 g unit for low values; to the nearest $\frac{1}{2}$ for foods which contain a lot of carbohydrate.

	Calories per 1 oz (30 g)	Calories per portion	Carbohydrate units per 1 oz (30 g)	Carbohydrate units per portion	Size of average portion

abalone

raw	30	30	0	0	1 oz (30 g)
steamed	25	125	0	0	5 oz (142 g)
canned	25	125	0	0	5 oz (142 g)
fried	35	175	0	0	5 oz (142 g)
ackee, canned	45	180	0	0	4 oz (114 g)
advocaat	75	75	3	3	1 oz (30 g)

ALCOHOLIC DRINKS

ale

brown, bottled	10	100	$\frac{1}{2}$	3	$\frac{1}{2}$ pt (284 ml)
pale, bottled	10	100	$\frac{1}{2}$	5	$\frac{1}{2}$ pt (284 ml)
strong	20	200	1	10	$\frac{1}{2}$ pt (284 ml)
anisette	65	65	3	3	1 oz (30 ml)
armagnac	65	65	3	3	1 oz (30 ml)
barley wine	20	200	1	10	$\frac{1}{2}$ pt (284 ml)

	Calories per 1 oz (30 g)	Calories per portion	Carbohydrate units per 1 oz (30 g)	Carbohydrate units per portion	Size of average portion
beer					
canned, bitter	10	100	$\frac{1}{2}$	5	$\frac{1}{2}$ pt (284 ml)
draught, bitter	10	100	$\frac{1}{2}$	5	$\frac{1}{2}$ pt (284 ml)
draught, mild	5	50	$\frac{1}{4}$	3	$\frac{1}{2}$ pt (284 ml)
benedictine	110	110	5	5	1 oz (30 ml)
blackcurrant liqueur	70	70	3	3	1 oz (30 ml)
Bloody Mary	30	210	$1\frac{1}{4}$	9	7 oz (199 ml)
bourbon	65	65	3	3	1 oz (30 ml)
calvados	70	70	3	3	1 oz (30 ml)
cassis	70	70	3	3	1 oz (30 ml)
champagne	20	80	1	4	4 oz (114 ml)
chartreuse	120	120	4	4	1 oz (30 ml)
cherry brandy	70	70	3	3	1 oz (30 ml)
cider					
dry	10	100	$\frac{1}{2}$	5	$\frac{1}{2}$ pt (284 ml)
sweet	10	100	$\frac{1}{2}$	5	$\frac{1}{2}$ pt (284 ml)
vintage	30	300	$1\frac{1}{2}$	10	$\frac{1}{2}$ pt (284 ml)
cognac	65	65	3	3	1 oz (30 ml)
cointreau	95	95	4	4	1 oz (30 ml)
crème de cacao	90	90	3	3	1 oz (30 ml)
crème de menthe	90	90	3	3	1 oz (30 ml)
curaçao	90	90	3	3	1 oz (30 ml)
gin	65	65	3	3	1 oz (30 ml)
grand marnier	90	90	3	3	1 oz (30 ml)

	Calories per 1 oz (30 g)	Calories per portion	Carbohydrate units per 1 oz (30 g)	Carbohydrate units per portion	Size of average portion
Irish coffee	40	200	1	5	$\frac{1}{4}$ pt (142 ml)
keg bitter	10	100	$\frac{1}{2}$	5	$\frac{1}{2}$ pt (284 ml)
kirsch	65	65	3	3	1 oz (30 ml)
lager, bottled	10	100	$\frac{1}{2}$	3	$\frac{1}{2}$ pt (284 ml)
madeira	35	35	$1\frac{1}{2}$	$1\frac{1}{2}$	1 oz (30 ml)
ouzo	65	65	3	3	1 oz (30 ml)
pastis	70	70	3	3	1 oz (30 ml)
port	45	90	2	4	2 oz (57 ml)
retsina	20	100	1	5	$\frac{1}{4}$ pt (142 ml)
rum					
white	65	65	3	3	1 oz (30 ml)
dark	65	65	3	3	1 oz (30 ml)
sangria	20	100	1	5	$\frac{1}{4}$ pt (142 ml)
schnapps	65	65	3	3	1 oz (30 ml)
screw driver	45	220	2	10	$\frac{1}{4}$ pt (142 ml)
shandy	10	80	$\frac{3}{4}$	4	$\frac{1}{2}$ pt (284 ml)
sherry					
dry	35	70	$1\frac{1}{2}$	3	2 oz (57 ml)
medium	35	70	$1\frac{3}{4}$	$3\frac{1}{2}$	2 oz (57 ml)
sweet	40	80	2	4	2 oz (57 ml)
stout	10	100	$\frac{1}{2}$	$5\frac{1}{2}$	$\frac{1}{2}$ pt (284 ml)
Tia Maria	90	90	3	3	1 oz (30 ml)
Tom Collins	25	250	$\frac{3}{4}$	8	$\frac{1}{2}$ pt (284 ml)
vermouth					
dry	35	70	2	4	2 oz (57 ml)

	Calories per 1 oz (30 g)	Calories per portion	Carbohydrate units per 1 oz (30 g)	Carbohydrate units per portion	Size of average portion
sweet	45	90	$2\frac{1}{2}$	5	2 oz (57 ml)
vodka	65	65	3	3	1 oz (30 ml)
vodka cocktail	50	160	2	6	3 oz (85 ml)
whisky	65	65	3	3	1 oz (30 ml)
whisky sour	55	240	$2\frac{1}{2}$	11	$4\frac{1}{2}$ oz (128 ml)
wine					
red	20	100	1	5	$\frac{1}{4}$ pt (142 ml)
rosé	20	100	1	5	$\frac{1}{4}$ pt (142 ml)
white, dry	20	100	1	5	$\frac{1}{4}$ pt (142 ml)
white, medium	20	100	1	5	$\frac{1}{4}$ pt (142 ml)
white, sweet	25	125	$1\frac{1}{2}$	7	$\frac{1}{4}$ pt (142 ml)
white, sparkling	20	100	1	5	$\frac{1}{4}$ pt (142 ml)
ale					
brown, bottled	10	100	$\frac{1}{2}$	3	$\frac{1}{2}$ pt (284 ml)
pale, bottled	10	100	$\frac{1}{2}$	5	$\frac{1}{2}$ pt (284 ml)
strong	20	200	1	10	$\frac{1}{2}$ pt (284 ml)
almonds	160	320	$\frac{1}{4}$	$\frac{1}{2}$	2 oz (57 g)
almond paste	125	125	3	3	1 oz (30 g)
anchovy					
raw	55	55	0	0	1 oz (30 g)
canned in oil or brine	55	55	0	0	1 oz (30 g)
anisette	65	65	3	3	1 oz (30 ml)
apples					
raw	10	60	$\frac{1}{2}$	$1\frac{1}{2}$	1 medium
chutney	55	55	3	3	1 oz (30 g)

	Calories per 1 oz (30 g)	Calories per portion	Carbohydrate units per 1 oz (30 g)	Carbohydrate units per portion	Size of average portion
cooking, raw	10	60	$\frac{1}{2}$	$1\frac{1}{2}$	1 medium
stewed, no sugar	10	50	$\frac{1}{2}$	$2\frac{1}{2}$	5 oz (142 g)
stewed + sugar	20	100	1	5	5 oz (142 g)
baked + sugar	10	60	$\frac{1}{2}$	$3\frac{1}{2}$	6 oz (171 g)
sauce	15	30	3	6	2 oz (57 g)
apple crumble	60	480	2	16	8 oz (227 g)
apples dried	65	65	$3\frac{1}{2}$	$3\frac{1}{2}$	1 oz (30 g)
apple juice, natural	15	65	$\frac{3}{4}$	$3\frac{1}{2}$	$\frac{1}{4}$ pt (142 ml)
apple pie	50	300	$1\frac{1}{2}$	$7\frac{1}{2}$	6 oz (171 g)
apricots					
raw	5	10	$\frac{1}{2}$	$\frac{1}{2}$	1 medium
stewed, no sugar	5	35	$\frac{1}{4}$	$1\frac{1}{2}$	5 oz (142 g)
stewed + sugar	15	85	1	$4\frac{1}{2}$	5 oz (142 g)
canned	30	120	$1\frac{1}{2}$	6	4 oz (114 g)
apricots, dried					
raw	50	50	$2\frac{1}{2}$	$2\frac{1}{2}$	1 oz (30 g)
stewed, no sugar	20	100	1	6	5 oz (142 g)
stewed + sugar	25	125	1	7	5 oz (142 g)
apricot jam	75	20	4	1	1 tsp
armagnac	65	65	3	3	1 oz (30 ml)
arrow root	100	100	$5\frac{1}{2}$	$5\frac{1}{2}$	1 oz (30 g)
artichokes					
globe, boiled	5	10	$\frac{1}{4}$	$\frac{1}{2}$	1 medium
heart, boiled	4	15	0	$\frac{1}{2}$	4 oz (114 g)
canned	4	15	0	$\frac{1}{2}$	4 oz (114 g)

	Calories per 1 oz (30 g)	Calories per portion	Carbohydrate units per 1 oz (30 g)	Carbohydrate units per portion	Size of average portion
Jerusalem, boiled	5	20	$\frac{1}{4}$	1	4 oz (114 g)
asparagus					
boiled	5	20	0	$\frac{1}{4}$	4 oz (114 g)
canned	3	10	0	$\frac{1}{4}$	4 oz (114 g)
aubergine					
fried	35	140	$\frac{1}{4}$	1	4 oz (114 g)
baked	25	100	$\frac{1}{4}$	1	4 oz (114 g)
Austrian smoked cheese	75	75	0	0	1 oz (30 g)
with ham	75	75	0	0	1 oz (30 g)
avocado pear	65	250	0	$\frac{1}{2}$	$\frac{1}{2}$ large

baby French cheese	90	90	0	0	1 oz (30 g)
bacon					
gammon joint					
raw	65	65	0	0	1 oz (30 g)

	Calories per 1 oz (30 g)	Calories per portion	Carbohydrate units per 1 oz (30 g)	Carbohydrate units per portion	Size of average portion
boiled	75	300	0	0	4 oz (114 g)
rashers, raw					
back	120	360	0	0	2 rashers
middle	120	360	0	0	2 rashers
streaky	120	240	0	0	2 rashers
rashers, fried					
back	130	260	0	0	2 rashers
middle	135	270	0	0	2 rashers
streaky	140	210	0	0	2 rashers
rashers, grilled					
back	115	160	0	0	2 rashers
middle	120	190	0	0	2 rashers
streaky	120	130	0	0	2 rashers
baked beans in tomato sauce	20	100	$\frac{1}{2}$	3	5 oz (142 g)
bamboo shoots, canned	10	10	$\frac{1}{4}$	$\frac{1}{4}$	1 oz (30 g)
banana, weighed with skin	15	75	$\frac{3}{4}$	3	1 medium
barley, pearl, boiled	35	35	2	2	1 oz (30 g)
barley wine	20	200	1	10	$\frac{1}{2}$ pt (284 ml)
bass					
raw	25	25	0	0	1 oz (30 g)
steamed	40	200	0	0	5 oz (142 g)

	Calories per 1 oz (30 g)	Calories per portion	Carbohydrate units per 1 oz (30 g)	Carbohydrate units per portion	Size of average portion
fried	50	250	o	o	5 oz (142 g)
beans					
French, boiled	2	10	o	o	5 oz (142 g)
runner, boiled	5	20	o	o	4 oz (114 g)
baked, in tomato sauce	20	100	$\frac{1}{2}$	3	5 oz (142 g)
broad, boiled	15	60	$\frac{1}{2}$	2	4 oz (114 g)
butter, boiled	25	100	I	4	4 oz (114 g)
haricot, boiled	25	100	I	4	4 oz (114 g)
mung, raw	65	65	2	2	1 oz (30 g)
cooked, dahl	30	60	$\frac{3}{4}$	$1\frac{1}{2}$	2 oz (57 g)
red kidney, boiled	25	100	I	4	4 oz (114 g)
soya, cooked	10	40	$\frac{1}{4}$	I	4 oz (114 g)
beansprouts					
raw	3	15	o	o	5 oz (142 g)
boiled	3	15	o	o	5 oz (142 g)
canned	5	25	o	o	5 oz (142 g)
béchamel sauce	40	160	$\frac{1}{2}$	2	4 oz (114 g)
beef					
lean, raw	35	35	o	o	1 oz (30 g)
fat, raw	180	180	o	o	1 oz (30 g)
brisket, boiled	95	380	o	o	4 oz (114 g)
corned	60	120	o	o	2 oz (57 g)
forerib, roast	100	400	o	o	4 oz (114 g)
joint, roast	100	400	o	o	4 oz (114 g)

	Calories per 1 oz (30 g)	Calories per portion	Carbohydrate units per 1 oz (30 g)	Carbohydrate units per portion	Size of average portion
minced					
lean raw	35	35	0	0	1 oz (30 g)
fat raw	65	65	0	0	1 oz (30 g)
stewed	65	260	0	0	4 oz (114 g)
silverside					
boiled	70	280	0	0	4 oz (114 g)
boiled, lean only	50	200	0	0	4 oz (114 g)
sirloin, roast	80	240	0	0	3 oz (85 g)
steak					
raw	55	55	0	0	1 oz (30 g)
grilled	55	330	0	0	6 oz (171 g) weighed raw
fried	65	390	0	0	6 oz (171 g) weighed raw
stewing steak					
raw	50	50	0	0	1 oz (30 g)
stewed	65	260	0	0	4 oz (114 g)
beefburgers					
fried	75	300	0	0	1 average
grilled	75	290	0	1	1 average
beef extract, concentrated	50	10	0	0	1 tsp
beef sausages					
fried	75	150	$\frac{1}{2}$	1	1 sausage
grilled	55	110	$\frac{1}{2}$	1	1 sausage

	Calories per 1 oz (30 g)	Calories per portion	Carbohydrate units per 1 oz (30 g)	Carbohydrate units per portion	Size of average portion
beef steak pudding	65	390	1	6	6 oz (171 g)
beef stew	35	340	$\frac{1}{4}$	2	10 oz (284 g)
beer					
canned bitter	10	100	$\frac{1}{2}$	5	$\frac{1}{2}$ pt (284 ml)
draught bitter	10	100	$\frac{1}{2}$	5	$\frac{1}{2}$ pt (284 ml)
draught mild	5	50	$\frac{1}{4}$	3	$\frac{1}{2}$ pt (284 ml)
beetroot	15	30	$\frac{1}{2}$	1	2 oz (57 g)
bel paese	80	80	0	0	1 oz (30 g)
benedictine	110	110	5	5	1 oz (30 ml)
Bengal gram					
raw	90	90	3	3	1 oz (30 g)
cooked (dahl)	40	80	1	2	2 oz (57 g)
bilberries, raw	15	65	$\frac{3}{4}$	3	4 oz (114 g)

BISCUITS AND BUNS

bourbon	120	60	3	$1\frac{1}{2}$	1 biscuit
butter biscuit	140	70	3	$1\frac{1}{2}$	1 biscuit
Chelsea bun	95	380	3	$11\frac{1}{2}$	1 bun
chocolate covered	150	120	4	$3\frac{1}{2}$	1 biscuit
coconut	100	50	3	$1\frac{1}{2}$	1 biscuit
cream crackers	125	40	4	$1\frac{1}{2}$	1 cracker
crispbread					
rye	90	25	4	1	1 biscuit
wheat starch reduced	110	30	2	$\frac{1}{2}$	1 biscuit

	Calories per 1 oz (30 g)	Calories per portion	Carbohydrate units per 1 oz (30 g)	Carbohydrate units per portion	Size of average portion
currant bun					
plain	85	340	3	$12\frac{1}{2}$	1 bun
iced	90	360	$3\frac{1}{2}$	$13\frac{1}{2}$	1 bun
custard cream	120	60	3	$1\frac{1}{2}$	1 biscuit
digestive					
plain	135	70	$3\frac{1}{2}$	2	1 biscuit
chocolate	140	130	$3\frac{1}{2}$	$3\frac{1}{2}$	1 biscuit
doughnut					
plain	105	420	$2\frac{1}{2}$	9	1 doughnut
with jam	115	450	3	11	1 doughnut
fruit shortcake	150	50	$4\frac{1}{2}$	$1\frac{1}{2}$	1 biscuit
gingernuts	130	65	$4\frac{1}{2}$	2	1 biscuit
grissini	85	15	$3\frac{1}{2}$	1	1 stick
hot cross bun	80	310	$2\frac{1}{2}$	10	1 bun
ice cream cone	75	25	15	5	1 cone
ice cream wafer	75	10	15	3	1 wafer
macaroon	100	200	$2\frac{1}{2}$	5	1 large
matzo	110	110	5	5	1 oz (30 g)
oatcakes	125	60	$3\frac{1}{2}$	2	1 biscuit
palmier	160	55	3	1	1 biscuit
rock bun	105	420	$3\frac{1}{2}$	14	1 bun
sandwich biscuit	145	95	4	$2\frac{1}{2}$	1 biscuit
semi sweet, e.g. rich tea	130	50	$4\frac{1}{2}$	$1\frac{1}{2}$	1 biscuit
shortbread	145	95	$3\frac{1}{2}$	$2\frac{1}{2}$	1 biscuit

	Calories per 1 oz (30 g)	Calories per portion	Carbohydrate units per 1 oz (30 g)	Carbohydrate units per portion	Size of average portion
sponge biscuit, chocolate covered	150	50	6	2	1 biscuit
sweet	135	55	$3\frac{1}{2}$	$1\frac{1}{2}$	1 biscuit
wafers filled	150	70	4	$1\frac{1}{2}$	1 wafer
water biscuit	125	60	$4\frac{1}{2}$	2	1 biscuit
bitter lemon	10	40	$\frac{1}{2}$	2	4 oz (114 ml)
blackberries					
raw	10	35	$\frac{1}{4}$	1	4 oz (114 g)
stewed, no sugar	5	30	$\frac{1}{4}$	1	4 oz (114 g)
stewed + sugar	15	65	$\frac{3}{4}$	$3\frac{1}{2}$	4 oz (114 g)
canned in syrup	15	65	$\frac{3}{4}$	$3\frac{1}{2}$	4 oz (114 g)
jam	75	20	4	1	1 tsp
black pudding, fried	90	350	$\frac{3}{4}$	$3\frac{1}{2}$	4 oz (114 g)
blackcurrants					
raw	10	35	$\frac{1}{4}$	1	4 oz (114 g)
stewed, no sugar	5	25	$\frac{1}{4}$	1	4 oz (114 g)
stewed + sugar	15	65	$\frac{3}{4}$	$3\frac{1}{2}$	4 oz (114 g)
canned in syrup	20	80	1	5	4 oz (114 g)
jam or jelly	75	20	4	1	1 tsp
juice, undiluted	65	65	$3\frac{1}{2}$	$3\frac{1}{2}$	1 oz (30 g)
blackcurrant liqueur	70	70	3	3	1 oz (30 ml)
blancmange	35	200	1	$6\frac{1}{2}$	6 oz (171 g)
bloater, grilled	70	420	0	0	6 oz (171 g)

	Calories per 1 oz (30 g)	Calories per portion	Carbohydrate units per 1 oz (30 g)	Carbohydrate units per portion	Size of average portion
Bloody Mary	30	210	$1\frac{1}{4}$	9	7 oz (199 ml)
boiled sweets	95	95	5	5	1 oz (30 g)
bolognese sauce	40	240	$\frac{1}{4}$	1	6 oz (171 g)
Bombay duck					
dried	70	25	0	0	1 fish
fried	120	40	0	0	1 fish
bourbon	65	65	3	3	1 oz (30 ml)
bourbon biscuit	120	60	3	$1\frac{1}{2}$	1 biscuit
brain					
calf, boiled	45	135	0	0	3 oz (85 g)
lamb, boiled	35	105	0	0	3 oz (85 g)
bran, millers'	55	20	$1\frac{1}{2}$	$\frac{1}{2}$	1 dsp
bran cereal	80	160	$2\frac{1}{2}$	5	2 oz (57 g)
bran flakes	100	100	$4\frac{1}{2}$	$4\frac{1}{2}$	1 oz (30 g)
bran wheat	60	20	$1\frac{1}{2}$	$\frac{1}{2}$	1 tbsp
brawn	45	90	0	0	2 oz (57 g)
Brazil nuts	175	350	$\frac{1}{4}$	$\frac{1}{2}$	2 oz (57 g)
bread					
bap	90	270	5	$9\frac{1}{2}$	1 medium
brown	65	65	$2\frac{1}{2}$	$2\frac{1}{2}$	1 oz (30 g)
croissant	105	260	$2\frac{1}{2}$	6	1 croissant
crumpet	75	110	2	3	1 crumpet
currant	70	70	3	3	1 oz (30 g)
granary	60	60	2	2	1 oz (30 g)
hovis	65	65	$2\frac{1}{2}$	$2\frac{1}{2}$	1 oz (30 g)

	Calories per 1 oz (30 g)	Calories per portion	Carbohydrate units per 1 oz (30 g)	Carbohydrate units per portion	Size of average portion
malt	70	70	3	3	1 oz (30 g)
muffins	65	130	3	$5\frac{1}{2}$	1 muffin
roll					
brown, crusty	80	160	$3\frac{1}{2}$	6	1 small
brown, soft	80	160	$2\frac{1}{2}$	5	1 small
white, crusty	80	160	$3\frac{1}{2}$	7	1 small
white, soft	85	170	3	6	1 small
starch-reduced	110	25	$2\frac{1}{2}$	$\frac{1}{2}$	1 roll
rye, light	70	70	3	3	1 oz (30 g)
rye, dark	90	90	$3\frac{1}{2}$	$3\frac{1}{2}$	1 oz (30 g)
soda	60	60	1	1	1 oz (30 g)
white	70	70	3	3	1 oz (30 g)
white, fried	65	65	3	3	1 oz (30 g)
white, toasted	85	85	$3\frac{1}{2}$	$3\frac{1}{2}$	1 oz (30 g)
white, crumbs, dried	100	100	$4\frac{1}{2}$	$4\frac{1}{2}$	1 oz (30 g)
wholemeal	60	60	$2\frac{1}{2}$	$2\frac{1}{2}$	1 oz (30 g)
bread sauce	30	60	$\frac{3}{4}$	$1\frac{1}{2}$	2 oz (57 g)

BREAKFAST CEREALS

bran cereals	80	160	$2\frac{1}{2}$	5	2 oz (57 g)
bran flakes	100	100	$4\frac{1}{2}$	$4\frac{1}{2}$	1 oz (30 g)
corn flakes	105	105	5	5	1 oz (30 g)
corn flakes, high-protein	110	55	$4\frac{1}{2}$	2	$\frac{1}{2}$ oz (14 g)

	Calories per 1 oz (30 g)	Calories per portion	Carbohydrate units per 1 oz (30 g)	Carbohydrate units per portion	Size of average portion
crisped rice	105	50	5	$2\frac{1}{2}$	$\frac{1}{2}$ oz (14 g)
flaked wheat biscuits	95	50	4	2	1 biscuit
grapenuts	100	100	$4\frac{1}{2}$	$4\frac{1}{2}$	1 oz (30 g)
instant porridge	110	110	4	4	1 oz (30 g)
muesli	105	210	4	8	2 oz (57 g)
puffed wheat	95	95	4	4	1 oz (30 g)
raisin bran	100	100	$4\frac{1}{2}$	$4\frac{1}{2}$	1 oz (30 g)
shredded wheat	90	90	4	4	1 oz (30 g)
sugar-coated puffed wheat	100	100	5	5	1 oz (30 g)
bream					
raw	25	25	0	0	1 oz (30 g)
steamed	40	190	0	0	5 oz (142 g)
fried	50	240	0	0	5 oz (142 g)
brie	85	85	0	0	1 oz (30 g)
brioche	90	220	2	5	1 roll
broad beans, boiled	15	60	$\frac{1}{2}$	2	4 oz (114 g)
broccoli tops, boiled	5	20	0	0	4 oz (114 g)
brown ale, bottled	10	100	$\frac{1}{2}$	3	$\frac{1}{2}$ pt (284 ml)
brown sauce, bottled	30	5	$1\frac{1}{2}$	$\frac{1}{2}$	1 tsp
Brussels sprouts, boiled	5	30	0	0	6 oz (171 g)

	Calories per 1 oz (30 g)	Calories per portion	Carbohydrate units per 1 oz (30 g)	Carbohydrate units per portion	Size of average portion
bun, currant					
plain	85	340	3	12½	1 bun
iced	90	360	3½	13½	1 bun
butter, salted & unsalted	210	50	0	0	1 pat
butter beans, boiled	25	100	1	4	4 oz (114 g)
butter biscuits	140	70	3	1½	1 biscuit
buttermilk	10	50	0	1	¼ pt (142 ml)

	Calories per 1 oz (30 g)	Calories per portion	Carbohydrate units per 1 oz (30 g)	Carbohydrate units per portion	Size of average portion
cabbage					
red raw	5	20	0	0	3 oz (85 g)
boiled	4	15	0	0	4 oz (114 g)
pickled	5	5	0	0	1 oz (30 g)
savoy, boiled	3	10	0	0	4 oz (114 g)

	Calories per 1 oz (30 g)	Calories per portion	Carbohydrate units per 1 oz (30 g)	Carbohydrate units per portion	Size of average portion
white, raw	3	10	0	0	4 oz (114 g)
white, boiled	4	15	0	0	4 oz (114 g)
caerphilly	100	100	0	0	1 oz (30 g)

CAKES AND PASTRIES

angel cake	60	240	$2\frac{1}{2}$	11	4 oz (114 g)
apple pie	50	300	$1\frac{1}{2}$	$7\frac{1}{2}$	6 oz (171 g)
apple strudel	60	230	$1\frac{1}{2}$	$6\frac{1}{2}$	4 oz (114 g)
bakewell tart	120	480	$2\frac{1}{2}$	10	4 oz (114 g)
battenburg cake	115	450	$2\frac{1}{2}$	10	4 oz (114 g)
cheese cake					
lemon	120	430	1	$4\frac{1}{2}$	4 oz (114 g)
currant	105	420	$1\frac{1}{2}$	5	4 oz (114 g)
cherry cake	90	350	2	7	4 oz (114 g)
chocolate cake iced, filled	85	330	$2\frac{1}{2}$	10	4 oz (114 g)
chocolate cup cake	115	230	3	6	1 cake
Christmas cake	90	360	3	12	4 oz (114 g)
custard tart	95	370	2	7	4 oz (114 g)
Danish pastry, apricot filling	105	210	$2\frac{1}{2}$	5	1 small
date & walnut loaf	80	310	3	$11\frac{1}{2}$	4 oz (114 g)
dumpling-suet	60	180	$1\frac{1}{2}$	$4\frac{1}{2}$	1 medium
Dundee cake	100	390	$2\frac{1}{2}$	11	4 oz (114 g)

	Calories per 1 oz (30 g)	Calories per portion	Carbohydrate units per 1 oz (30 g)	Carbohydrate units per portion	Size of average portion
eccles	75	150	2	4	1 small
éclair	105	210	2	4	1 small
fairy	105	105	$3\frac{1}{2}$	$3\frac{1}{2}$	1 small
fancy iced cake	115	230	4	8	1 cake
fruit cake					
rich	95	280	3	9	3 oz (85 g)
iced	100	300	$3\frac{1}{2}$	10	3 oz (85 g)
plain	100	300	3	9	3 oz (85 g)
gingerbread	105	315	$3\frac{1}{2}$	10	3 oz (85 g)
jam tart	120	120	$3\frac{1}{2}$	$3\frac{1}{2}$	1 tart
lardy cake	105	410	$3\frac{1}{2}$	$14\frac{1}{2}$	4 oz (114 g)
madeira cake	110	330	$3\frac{1}{2}$	10	3 oz (85 g)
meringue	110	50	$5\frac{1}{2}$	$2\frac{1}{2}$	1 large
mince pie	125	210	$3\frac{1}{2}$	6	1 pie
pastry, choux					
raw	60	60	1	1	1 oz (30 g)
cooked	95	95	$1\frac{1}{2}$	$1\frac{1}{2}$	1 oz (30 g)
pastry, flaky					
raw	120	120	2	2	1 oz (30 g)
cooked	160	160	$2\frac{1}{2}$	$2\frac{1}{2}$	1 oz (30 g)
pastry, short					
raw	130	130	$2\frac{1}{2}$	$2\frac{1}{2}$	1 oz (30 g)
cooked	150	150	3	3	1 oz (30 g)
scones					
plain	85	130	$2\frac{1}{2}$	4	1 medium

	Calories per 1 oz (30 g)	Calories per portion	Carbohydrate units per 1 oz (30 g)	Carbohydrate units per portion	Size of average portion
cheese	100	200	$2\frac{1}{2}$	$4\frac{1}{2}$	1 medium
currant	105	160	$3\frac{1}{2}$	5	1 medium
scotch pancakes, without butter	80	120	2	3	1 medium
sponge cake					
with fat	130	260	3	6	2 oz (57 g)
fatless	85	170	3	6	2 oz (57 g)
with jam	85	170	$3\frac{1}{2}$	7	2 oz (57 g)
simnel cake	110	440	3	12	4 oz (114 g)
Swiss roll	75	290	3	12	4 oz (114 g)
tea cake	85	170	3	6	1 tea cake
treacle tart	105	420	$3\frac{1}{2}$	14	4 oz (114 g)
calvados	70	70	3	3	1 oz (30 ml)
camembert	85	85	0	0	1 oz (30 g)
capers	0	0	0	0	1 oz (30 g)
carp					
raw	25	25	0	0	1 oz (30 g)
steamed	40	190	0	0	5 oz (142 g)
fried	50	240	0	0	5 oz (142 g)
carrots					
old, raw	5	20	$\frac{1}{4}$	1	4 oz (114 g)
old, boiled	5	20	$\frac{1}{4}$	1	4 oz (114 g)
young, raw	5	30	$\frac{1}{2}$	1	4 oz (114 g)
young, boiled	4	15	$\frac{1}{4}$	1	4 oz (114 g)
young, canned	5	20	$\frac{1}{4}$	1	4 oz (114 g)

	Calories per 1 oz (30 g)	Calories per portion	Carbohydrate units per 1 oz (30 g)	Carbohydrate units per portion	Size of average portion
carrot juice	5	25	$\frac{1}{2}$	2	$\frac{1}{4}$ pt (142 ml)
cashew nuts	155	610	1	$3\frac{1}{2}$	4 oz (114 g)
cassata	45	95	$1\frac{1}{2}$	3	2 oz (57 g)
cassis	70	70	3	3	1 oz (30 ml)
cauliflower					
raw	4	15	0	0	4 oz (114 g)
boiled	3	10	0	0	4 oz (114 g)
pickled	3	3	0	0	1 oz (30 g)
cauliflower cheese	30	255	$\frac{1}{4}$	2	8 oz (227 g)
caviar					
red	60	60	0	0	1 oz (30 g)
black	60	60	0	0	1 oz (30 g)
grey	60	60	0	0	1 oz (30 g)
celeriac					
raw	5	10	0	0	2 oz (57 g)
boiled	4	15	0	0	4 oz (114 g)
celery					
raw	2	5	0	0	2 oz (57 g)
boiled	2	5	0	0	2 oz (57 g)
canned	1	5	0	0	4 oz (114 g)
champagne	20	80	1	4	4 oz (114 ml)
chapatis					
with fat	95	475	3	15	1 large
fatless	60	285	$2\frac{1}{2}$	$12\frac{1}{2}$	1 large
chartreuse	120	120	4	4	1 oz (30 ml)

	Calories per 1 oz (30 g)	Calories per portion	Carbohydrate units per 1 oz (30 g)	Carbohydrate units per portion	Size of average portion
CHEESE					
Austrian smoked	75	75	o	o	1 oz (30 g)
with ham	75	75	o	o	1 oz (30 g)
baby French, soft	90	90	o	o	1 oz (30 g)
bel paese	80	80	o	o	1 oz (30 g)
boursin					
with herbs	110	110	o	o	1 oz (30 g)
with pepper	110	110	o	o	1 oz (30 g)
caerphilly	100	100	o	o	1 oz (30 g)
camembert	85	85	o	o	1 oz (30 g)
cheddar	120	120	o	o	1 oz (30 g)
cheshire	120	120	o	o	1 oz (30 g)
cottage cheese					
plain	25	100	o	o	small carton
+ chives	25	100	o	o	small carton
+ onions & peppers	25	100	o	o	small carton
+ pineapple	25	100	o	1	small carton
cream	125	125	o	o	1 oz (30 g)
danbo	95	95	o	o	1 oz (30 g)
Danish blue	100	100	o	o	1 oz (30 g)
dolcelatte	95	95	o	o	1 oz (30 g)
double gloucester	100	100	o	o	1 oz (30 g)
edam	85	85	o	o	1 oz (30 g)
emmenthal	110	110	o	o	1 oz (30 g)
esrom	90	90	o	o	1 oz (30 g)

	Calories per 1 oz (30 g)	Calories per portion	Carbohydrate units per 1 oz (30 g)	Carbohydrate units per portion	Size of average portion
gorgonzola	100	100	0	0	1 oz (30 g)
gouda	85	85	0	0	1 oz (30 g)
gruyère	130	130	0	0	1 oz (30 g)
lancashire	100	100	0	0	1 oz (30 g)
leicester	110	110	0	0	1 oz (30 g)
mozzarella	95	95	0	0	1 oz (30 g)
parmesan	120	20	0	0	2 tsp
Port Salut	90	90	0	0	1 oz (30 g)
processed	90	90	0	0	1 oz (30 g)
ricotta	70	70	0	0	1 oz (30 g)
roquefort	100	100	0	0	1 oz (30 g)
sage derby	110	110	0	0	1 oz (30 g)
St. Paulin	90	90	0	0	1 oz (30 g)
stilton blue	130	130	0	0	1 oz (30 g)
tomé au raisin	80	80	0	0	1 oz (30 g)
wensleydale	110	110	0	0	1 oz (30 g)
cheese cake					
lemon	120	430	1	$4\frac{1}{2}$	4 oz (114 g)
currant	105	420	$1\frac{1}{2}$	5	4 oz (114 g)
cheese football	150	15	5	$\frac{1}{2}$	1 football
cheese pudding	50	300	$\frac{1}{2}$	3	6 oz (171 g)
cheese sauce	55	280	$\frac{1}{2}$	$2\frac{1}{2}$	5 oz (142 g)
cheese soufflé	70	355	$\frac{1}{2}$	3	5 oz (142 g)
cheese spread	80	80	0	0	1 portion
cheese straws	160	160	$1\frac{1}{2}$	$1\frac{1}{2}$	1 oz (30 g)

	Calories per 1 oz (30 g)	Calories per portion	Carbohydrate units per 1 oz (30 g)	Carbohydrate units per portion	Size of average portion
chelsea bun	95	380	3	$11\frac{1}{2}$	1 bun
cherries					
eating, raw	10	45	$\frac{1}{2}$	2	4 oz (114 g)
cooking, raw	10	45	$\frac{1}{2}$	2	4 oz (114 g)
stewed, no sugar	10	45	$\frac{1}{2}$	2	4 oz (114 g)
stewed + sugar	20	80	1	4	4 oz (114 g)
canned	20	80	1	4	4 oz (114 g)
glacé	60	10	3	$\frac{1}{2}$	1 cherry
cherry jam	75	20	4	1	1 tsp
cherry brandy	70	70	3	3	1 oz (30 ml)
cheshire cheese	120	120	0	0	1 oz (30 g)
chestnuts	50	100	2	4	2 oz (57 g)
chickpeas					
raw	90	90	3	3	1 oz (30 g)
cooked, dahl	40	160	1	4	4 oz (114 g)
chicken					
raw, meat only	35	35	0	0	1 oz (30 g)
raw, meat & skin	65	65	0	0	1 oz (30 g)
boiled					
meat only	50	255	0	0	5 oz (142 g)
light meat	45	230	0	0	5 oz (142 g)
dark meat	60	295	0	0	5 oz (142 g)
roast					
meat only	40	210	0	0	5 oz (142 g)
meat & skin	60	290	0	0	5 oz (142 g)

	Calories per 1 oz (30 g)	Calories per portion	Carbohydrate units per 1 oz (30 g)	Carbohydrate units per portion	Size of average portion
light meat	40	200	0	0	5 oz (142 g)
dark meat	45	220	0	0	5 oz (142 g)
wing quarter	20	65	0	0	1 medium
leg quarter	25	155	0	0	1 small
chicken cream soup	15	140	0	2	$\frac{1}{2}$ pt (284 ml)
chicken noodle soup	5	55	0	2	$\frac{1}{2}$ pt (284 ml)
chicory					
raw	3	5	0	0	2 oz (57 g)
boiled	3	10	0	0	4 oz (114 g)
chips, potato					
fresh	70	430	2	12	6 oz (171 g)
frozen	80	495	2	10	6 oz (171 g)
chocolate					
milk	150	250	$3\frac{1}{2}$	6	small bar
plain	150	250	$3\frac{1}{2}$	6	small bar
fancy	130	520	4	15	4 oz (114 g)
drinking	105	35	4	$1\frac{1}{2}$	2 tsp
biscuit, full coated	150	120	4	$3\frac{1}{2}$	1 biscuit
chocolate ice cream	45	95	$1\frac{1}{2}$	3	2 oz (57 g)
chocolate malted milk powder	105	35	$4\frac{1}{2}$	$1\frac{1}{2}$	1 tsp
chocolate mousse, frozen	35	100	1	3	$3\frac{1}{2}$ oz (100 g)
choux pastry					
raw	60	60	1	1	1 oz (30 g)

	Calories per 1 oz (30 g)	Calories per portion	Carbohydrate units per 1 oz (30 g)	Carbohydrate units per portion	Size of average portion
cooked	95	95	$1\frac{1}{2}$	$1\frac{1}{2}$	1 oz (30 g)
Christmas cake	90	360	3	12	4 oz (114 g)
Christmas pudding	85	340	$2\frac{1}{2}$	10	4 oz (114 g)
chutney					
apple	55	55	3	3	1 oz (30 g)
mango	55	55	3	3	1 oz (30 g)
tomato	45	45	2	2	1 oz (30 g)
cider					
dry	10	100	$\frac{1}{2}$	5	$\frac{1}{2}$ pt (284 ml)
sweet	10	100	$\frac{1}{2}$	5	$\frac{1}{2}$ pt (284 ml)
vintage	30	300	$1\frac{1}{2}$	10	$\frac{1}{2}$ pt (284 ml)
clam					
raw	20	20	0	0	1 oz (30 g)
steamed	30	60	0	0	2 oz (57 g)
canned	30	60	0	0	2 oz (57 g)
clementine	10	10	$\frac{1}{2}$	$\frac{1}{2}$	1 small
clotted cream	160	160	0	0	1 oz (30 g)
cockles					
shelled, raw	10	10	0	0	1 oz (30 g)
boiled	15	30	0	0	2 oz (57 g)
canned	15	30	0	0	2 oz (57 g)
cocoa powder	90	15	$\frac{3}{4}$	0	1 tsp
coconut					
desiccated	175	175	$1\frac{1}{2}$	$1\frac{1}{2}$	1 oz (30 g)
fresh	100	100	$\frac{1}{4}$	$\frac{1}{4}$	1 oz (30 g)

	Calories per 1 oz (30 g)	Calories per portion	Carbohydrate units per 1 oz (30 g)	Carbohydrate units per portion	Size of average portion
milk	5	10	$\frac{1}{4}$	$\frac{1}{2}$	2 oz (57 g)
oil	255	255	0	0	1 oz (30 g)
coconut biscuit	100	50	3	$1\frac{1}{2}$	1 biscuit
cod					
raw	20	20	0	0	1 oz (30 g)
steamed	25	130	0	0	5 oz (142 g)
fried	35	180	0	0	5 oz (142 g)
fried in batter	55	340	$\frac{1}{2}$	2	6 oz (171 g)
fried in breadcrumbs	50	300	0	0	6 oz (171 g)
cod roe					
fried	55	110	$\frac{3}{4}$	$1\frac{1}{2}$	2 oz (57 g)
smoked	30	30	0	0	1 oz (30 g)
cod liver oil	255	40	0	0	1 tsp
coffee & chicory essence	60	10	3	$\frac{1}{2}$	1 tsp
coffee ground with water	0	2	0	0	1 cup
coffee instant	30	1	0	0	1 tsp
coffee Irish	40	200	1	5	$\frac{1}{4}$ pt (142 ml)
cognac	65	65	3	3	1 oz (30 ml)
cointreau	85	95	4	4	1 oz (30 ml)
cola drink	10	110	$\frac{1}{2}$	5	$\frac{1}{2}$ pt (284 ml)
coleslaw	20	70	0	1	4 oz (114 g)
condensed milk					
whole, sweetened	90	90	3	3	1 oz (30 ml)

	Calories per 1 oz (30 g)	Calories per portion	Carbohydrate units per 1 oz (30 g)	Carbohydrate units per portion	Size of average portion
skimmed, sweetened	75	75	$3\frac{1}{2}$	$3\frac{1}{2}$	1 oz (30 ml)
consommé	10	70	0	0	$\frac{1}{2}$ pt (284 ml)
corn oil	255	255	0	0	1 oz (30 ml)
corn on cob, boiled	35	175	1	6	1 medium
corned beef	60	120	0	0	2 oz (57 g)
corn flakes	105	105	5	5	1 oz (30 g)
cornflour	100	15	5	1	1 tsp
cornish pasty	95	570	2	11	6 oz (171 g)
cottage cheese					
plain	25	100	0	0	small carton
+ chives	25	100	0	0	small carton
+ onions & pepper	25	100	0	0	small carton
+ pineapple	25	100	0	1	small carton
courgette					
raw	3	3	0	0	1 oz (30 g)
boiled	1	5	0	0	4 oz (114 g)
fried	35	140	0	$\frac{1}{2}$	4 oz (114 g)
crab					
boiled	35	140	0	0	4 oz (114 g)
canned	25	100	0	0	4 oz (114 g)
cranberries					
raw	4	4	$\frac{1}{4}$	$\frac{1}{4}$	1 oz (30 g)
sauce or jelly	40	20	2	1	1 dsp
crayfish					
in shells	10	70	0	0	6 oz (171 g)

	Calories per 1 oz (30 g)	Calories per portion	Carbohydrate units per 1 oz (30 g)	Carbohydrate units per portion	Size of average portion
shelled	30	60	0	0	2 oz (57 g)
cream					
clotted	160	160	0	0	1 oz (30 ml)
double	125	510	0	0	small carton
single	60	240	$\frac{1}{4}$	1	small carton
soured	55	55	0	0	1 oz (30 ml)
sterilized	65	65	$\frac{1}{4}$	$\frac{1}{4}$	1 oz (30 ml)
whipping	95	95	0	0	1 oz (30 ml)
cream cheese	125	125	0	0	1 oz (30 ml)
cream crackers	125	40	4	$1\frac{1}{2}$	1 cracker
crème de cacao	90	90	3	3	1 oz (30 ml)
crème de menthe	90	90	3	3	1 oz (30 ml)
crispbread					
rye	90	25	4	1	1 biscuit
starch reduced	110	30	2	$\frac{1}{2}$	1 biscuit
crisped rice breakfast cereal	105	50	5	$2\frac{1}{2}$	$\frac{1}{2}$ oz (14 g)
crisps, potato	150	125	3	$2\frac{1}{2}$	small pkt
croissant	105	260	$2\frac{1}{2}$	6	1 croissant
crumpet	75	110	2	3	1 crumpet
cucumber					
raw	3	3	0	0	1 oz (30 g)
pickled	3	3	$\frac{1}{4}$	$\frac{1}{4}$	1 oz (30 g)
curaçao	90	90	3	3	1 oz (30 ml)
curd cheese	25	25	0	0	1 oz (30 g)

	Calories per 1 oz (30 g)	Calories per portion	Carbohydrate units per 1 oz (30 g)	Carbohydrate units per portion	Size of average portion
currant bun					
plain	85	340	3	$12\frac{1}{2}$	1 bun
iced	90	360	$3\frac{1}{2}$	$13\frac{1}{2}$	1 bun
curried meat	45	270	$\frac{1}{2}$	$2\frac{1}{2}$	6 oz (171 g)
curry powder	65	65	$1\frac{1}{2}$	$1\frac{1}{2}$	1 oz (30 g)
custard, egg	35	135	$\frac{1}{2}$	$2\frac{1}{2}$	4 oz (114 g)
custard cream biscuit	120	60	3	$1\frac{1}{2}$	1 biscuit
custard powder	100	100	5	5	1 oz (30 g)
boiled	35	170	1	5	5 oz (142 g)
custard tart	95	370	2	7	4 oz (114 g)

dahl (cooked chickpeas)	40	160	1	4	4 oz (114 g)
dahl (cooked mung beans)	30	60	$\frac{3}{4}$	$1\frac{1}{2}$	2 oz (57 g)

	Calories per 1 oz (30 g)	Calories per portion	Carbohydrate units per 1 oz (30 g)	Carbohydrate units per portion	Size of average portion
dahl, masur (cooked lentils)	25	105	$\frac{3}{4}$	$2\frac{1}{2}$	4 oz (114 g)
damsons					
raw	10	40	$\frac{1}{2}$	2	4 oz (114 g)
stewed, no sugar	10	40	$\frac{1}{2}$	2	4 oz (114 g)
stewed + sugar	20	80	1	4	4 oz (114 g)
danbo cheese	95	95	0	0	1 oz (30 g)
Danish blue cheese	100	100	0	0	1 oz (30 g)
Danish pastry, apricot filling	105	210	$2\frac{1}{2}$	5	1 small
dates, dried	60	120	3	6	2 oz (57 g)
date & walnut loaf	80	310	3	$11\frac{1}{2}$	4 oz (114 g)
desiccated coconut	175	175	$1\frac{1}{2}$	$1\frac{1}{2}$	1 oz (30 g)
digestive biscuit					
chocolate	140	130	$3\frac{1}{2}$	$3\frac{1}{2}$	1 biscuit
plain	135	70	$3\frac{1}{2}$	2	1 biscuit
dogfish, fried in batter	75	375	$\frac{1}{2}$	2	5 oz (142 g)
dolcelatte cheese	95	95	0	0	1 oz (30 g)
double gloucester cheese	100	100	0	0	1 oz (30 g)
doughnuts					
plain	105	420	$2\frac{1}{2}$	9	1 doughnut
with jam	115	450	3	11	1 doughnut
drambuie	65	65	3	3	1 oz (30 ml)

	Calories per 1 oz (30 g)	Calories per portion	Carbohydrate units per 1 oz (30 g)	Carbohydrate units per portion	Size of average portion
dried milk					
whole	140	35	2	$\frac{1}{2}$	2 tsp
skimmed	100	15	3	$\frac{1}{2}$	2 tsp
drinking chocolate	105	35	4	$1\frac{1}{2}$	2 tsp
dripping, beef	255	255	0	0	1 oz (30 g)
drop scones	80	120	2	3	1 small
duck					
raw meat only	35	35	0	0	1 oz (30 g)
roast meat only	55	270	0	0	5 oz (142 g)
dumpling-suet	60	180	$1\frac{1}{2}$	$4\frac{1}{2}$	1 medium
Dundee cake	100	390	$2\frac{1}{2}$	11	4 oz (114 g)

eccles cake	75	150	2	4	1 small
éclairs	105	210	2	4	1 small
edam cheese	85	85	0	0	1 oz (30 g)

	Calories per 1 oz (30 g)	Calories per portion	Carbohydrate units per 1 oz (30 g)	Carbohydrate units per portion	Size of average portion
eel					
raw	50	50	0	0	1 oz (30 g)
fried	70	340	0	0	5 oz (142 g)
fried in batter	70	350	$\frac{1}{4}$	$1\frac{1}{2}$	6 oz (171 g)
jellied	60	230	0	0	4 oz (114 g)
smoked	55	110	0	0	2 oz (57 g)
steamed	55	280	0	0	5 oz (142 g)
egg custard	35	135	$\frac{1}{2}$	$2\frac{1}{2}$	4 oz (114 g)
eggplant					
fried	35	140	$\frac{1}{4}$	1	4 oz (114 g)
baked	25	100	$\frac{1}{4}$	1	4 oz (114 g)
egg					
whole, raw	40	80	0	0	1 large
white, raw	10	15	0	0	1 large
yolk, raw	95	80	0	0	1 large
whole, boiled	40	80	0	0	1 large
whole, fried	65	130	0	0	1 large
whole, poached	45	90	0	0	1 large
scrambled	70	140	0	0	1 large
emmenthal cheese	110	110	0	0	1 oz (30 g)
endive					
raw	3	5	0	0	2 oz (57 g)
boiled	3	10	0	0	4 oz (114 g)
evaporated milk, whole, unsweetened	45	45	$\frac{3}{4}$	$\frac{3}{4}$	1 oz (30 ml)

	Calories per 1 oz (30 g)	Calories per portion	Carbohydrate units per 1 oz (30 g)	Carbohydrate units per portion	Size of average portion
faggots	75	600	$\frac{3}{4}$	7	2 faggots
fairy cake	105	105	$3\frac{1}{2}$	$3\frac{1}{2}$	1 small
fancy iced cakes	115	230	4	8	1 small
figs					
green, raw	10	15	$\frac{3}{4}$	1	1 fig
dried, raw	60	45	3	$2\frac{1}{2}$	1 fig
stewed, no sugar	35	170	$1\frac{1}{2}$	8	5 oz (142 g)
stewed + sugar	40	195	2	10	5 oz (142 g)

FISH

abalone

raw	30	30	0	0	1 oz (30 g)
steamed	25	125	0	0	5 oz (142 g)

	Calories per 1 oz (30 g)	Calories per portion	Carbohydrate units per 1 oz (30 g)	Carbohydrate units per portion	Size of average portion
canned	25	125	0	0	5 oz (142 g)
fried	35	175	0	0	5 oz (142 g)
anchovy					
raw	55	55	0	0	1 oz (30 g)
canned in oil or brine	55	55	0	0	1 oz (30 g)
bass					
raw	25	25	0	0	1 oz (30 g)
steamed	40	200	0	0	5 oz (142 g)
fried	50	250	0	0	5 oz (142 g)
bloater, grilled	70	420	0	0	6 oz (171 g)
Bombay duck					
dried	70	25	0	0	1 fish
fried	120	40	0	0	1 fish
bream					
raw	25	25	0	0	1 oz (30 g)
steamed	40	190	0	0	5 oz (142 g)
fried	50	240	0	0	5 oz (142 g)
carp					
raw	25	25	0	0	1 oz (30 g)
steamed	40	190	0	0	5 oz (142 g)
fried	50	240	0	0	5 oz (142 g)
caviar					
red, black, grey	60	60	0	0	1 oz (30 g)
clam					
raw	20	20	0	0	1 oz (30 g)

	Calories per 1 oz (30 g)	Calories per portion	Carbohydrate units per 1 oz (30 g)	Carbohydrate units per portion	Size of average portion
steamed	30	60	0	0	5 oz (142 g)
canned	30	60	0	0	5 oz (142 g)
cockles					
shelled, raw	10	10	0	0	1 oz (30 g)
boiled	15	30	0	0	2 oz (57 g)
canned	15	30	0	0	2 oz (57 g)
cod					
raw	20	20	0	0	1 oz (30 g)
steamed	25	130	0	0	5 oz (142 g)
fried	35	180	0	0	5 oz (142 g)
fried in batter	55	340	$\frac{1}{2}$	2	6 oz (171 g)
in breadcrumbs	50	300	0	0	6 oz (171 g)
cod roe					
fried	55	110	$\frac{3}{4}$	$1\frac{1}{2}$	2 oz (57 g)
smoked	30	30	0	0	1 oz (30 g)
crab					
boiled	35	140	0	0	4 oz (114 g)
canned	25	100	0	0	4 oz (114 g)
crayfish					
in shells	10	70	0	0	6 oz (171 g)
shelled	30	60	0	0	6 oz (171 g)
dogfish fried in batter	75	375	$\frac{1}{2}$	2	5 oz (142 g)
eel					
raw	50	50	0	0	1 oz (30 g)

	Calories per 1 oz (30 g)	Calories per portion	Carbohydrate units per 1 oz (30 g)	Carbohydrate units per portion	Size of average portion
fried	70	340	0	0	5 oz (142 g)
fried in batter	70	350	$\frac{1}{4}$	$1\frac{1}{2}$	6 oz (171 g)
jellied	60	230	0	0	4 oz (114 g)
smoked	55	110	0	0	2 oz (57 g)
steamed	55	280	0	0	5 oz (142 g)
haddock					
fresh, raw	20	20	0	0	1 oz (30 g)
fried	50	250	0	0	5 oz (142 g)
steamed	30	150	0	0	5 oz (142 g)
smoked, raw	20	20	0	0	1 oz (30 g)
steamed	30	145	0	0	5 oz (142 g)
hake					
raw	20	20	0	0	1 oz (30 g)
poached	30	150	0	0	5 oz (142 g)
halibut					
raw	25	25	0	0	1 oz (30 g)
steamed	35	185	0	0	5 oz (142 g)
poached	40	190	0	0	5 oz (142 g)
fried	50	240	0	0	5 oz (142 g)
herring					
raw	65	65	0	0	1 oz (30 g)
steamed	55	280	0	0	5 oz (142 g)
fried in oatmeal	65	330	0	$\frac{1}{2}$	5 oz (142 g)
pickled	80	160	0	0	2 oz (57 g)
roe, fried	70	140	$\frac{1}{4}$	$\frac{1}{2}$	2 oz (57 g)

	Calories per 1 oz (30 g)	Calories per portion	Carbohydrate units per 1 oz (30 g)	Carbohydrate units per portion	Size of average portion
kipper					
raw	80	80	0	0	1 oz (30 g)
baked or steamed	60	290	0	0	5 oz (142 g)
fried	70	340	0	0	5 oz (142 g)
lobster, boiled	35	175	0	0	5 oz (142 g)
mackerel					
raw	65	65	0	0	1 oz (30 g)
fried	55	275	0	0	5 oz (142 g)
steamed	75	380	0	0	5 oz (142 g)
smoked	90	440	0	0	5 oz (142 g)
mullet					
raw	40	40	0	0	1 oz (30 g)
steamed	50	250	0	0	5 oz (142 g)
fried	60	300	0	0	5 oz (142 g)
mussels					
raw	20	20	0	0	1 oz (30 g)
steamed	25	75	0	0	3 oz (85 g)
canned	20	55	0	0	3 oz (85 g)
octopus					
raw	20	20	0	0	1 oz (30 g)
steamed	25	125	0	0	5 oz (142 g)
fried	30	160	0	0	5 oz (142 g)
fried in batter	55	340	$\frac{1}{2}$	$2\frac{1}{2}$	5 oz (142 g)
oyster					
raw	15	15	0	0	2 oysters

	Calories per 1 oz (30 g)	Calories per portion	Carbohydrate units per 1 oz (30 g)	Carbohydrate units per portion	Size of average portion
canned	15	45	o	o	6 oysters
smoked	15	45	o	o	3 oz (85 g)
pilchards					
canned in oil	65	250	o	o	4 oz (114 g)
canned in tomato					
sauce	35	140	o	$\frac{1}{4}$	4 oz (114 g)
plaice					
raw	25	25	o	o	1 oz (30 g)
steamed	25	130	o	o	5 oz (142 g)
fried in batter	80	400	$\frac{3}{4}$	4	5 oz (142 g)
fried in breadcrumbs	65	325	$\frac{1}{2}$	$2\frac{1}{2}$	5 oz (142 g)
prawns					
raw in shells	10	10	o	o	1 oz (30 g)
shelled	30	60	o	o	2 oz (57 g)
boiled	30	60	o	o	2 oz (57 g)
potted	120	240	o	o	2 oz (57 g)
salmon					
raw	50	50	o	o	1 oz (30 g)
steamed	55	280	o	o	5 oz (142 g)
fried	65	330	o	o	5 oz (142 g)
smoked	40	80	o	o	2 oz (57 g)
canned	45	90	o	o	2 oz (57 g)
salmon trout					
raw	50	50	o	o	1 oz (30 g)
poached	55	280	o	o	5 oz (142 g)

	Calories per 1 oz (30 g)	Calories per portion	Carbohydrate units per 1 oz (30 g)	Carbohydrate units per portion	Size of average portion
sardine					
canned in oil, drained	60	120	0	0	2 oz (57 g)
canned in tomato sauce	50	100	0	0	2 oz (57 g)
scallop					
raw	30	30	0	0	1 oz (30 g)
steamed	30	90	0	0	2 fish
fried	35	115	0	0	2 fish
canned	30	90	0	0	3 oz (85 g)
scampi					
boiled	30	120	0	0	3 pieces
fried in batter	55	275	$\frac{1}{2}$	2	3 pieces
fried in breadcrumbs	90	450	2	8	3 pieces
skate					
raw	20	20	0	0	1 oz (30 g)
steamed	25	130	0	0	5 oz (142 g)
fried	35	180	0	0	5 oz (142 g)
fried in batter	55	340	$\frac{1}{2}$	3	6 oz (171 g)
fried in breadcrumbs	50	350	$\frac{1}{4}$	1	6 oz (171 g)
sole, lemon					
raw	25	25	0	0	1 oz (30 g)
steamed	25	130	0	0	5 oz (142 g)
fried in breadcrumbs	60	310	0	$\frac{1}{2}$	5 oz (142 g)
sprats					
raw	25	25	0	0	1 oz (30 g)

	Calories per 1 oz (30 g)	Calories per portion	Carbohydrate units per 1 oz (30 g)	Carbohydrate units per portion	Size of average portion
fried	125	500	0	0	4 oz (114 g)
fried in batter	125	500	$\frac{1}{2}$	2	4 oz (114 g)
squid					
raw	20	20	0	0	1 oz (30 g)
steamed	25	125	0	0	5 oz (142 g)
fried	35	170	0	0	5 oz (142 g)
trout					
raw	25	25	0	0	1 oz (30 g)
steamed	25	200	0	0	1 small
fried	40	320	0	0	1 small
smoked	25	200	0	0	1 small
tuna in oil, drained	80	160	0	0	1 small can
turbot					
raw	20	20	0	0	1 oz (30 g)
steamed	30	140	0	0	5 oz (142 g)
fried in breadcrumbs	50	250	$\frac{1}{4}$	1	5 oz (142 g)
whitebait					
raw	15	15	0	0	1 oz (30 g)
fried in batter	150	590	$\frac{1}{2}$	2	4 oz (114 g)
fried in flour	150	590	$\frac{1}{4}$	1	4 oz (114 g)
whiting					
fried	55	275	$\frac{1}{2}$	2	5 oz (142 g)
steamed	25	130	0	0	5 oz (142 g)
winkles					
boiled in shell	4	4	0	0	1 oz (30 g)

	Calories per 1 oz (30 g)	Calories per portion	Carbohydrate units per 1 oz (30 g)	Carbohydrate units per portion	Size of average portion
shelled	20	60	0	0	3 oz (85 g)
fish cakes					
frozen	30	60	1	2	1 cake
fried	65	130	1	2	1 cake
fish fingers					
frozen	50	100	1	2	2 fingers
fried	65	130	1	2	2 fingers
fish paste	50	10	$\frac{1}{4}$	0	1 tsp
fish pie	35	280	$\frac{3}{4}$	6	8 oz (227 g)
flaked wheat biscuits	95	50	4	2	1 biscuit
flaky pastry					
raw	120	120	$2\frac{1}{2}$	$2\frac{1}{2}$	1 oz (30 g)
cooked	160	160	$2\frac{1}{2}$	$2\frac{1}{2}$	1 oz (30 g)
flour					
brown	95	95	4	4	1 oz (30 g)
white bread-making	95	95	4	4	1 oz (30 g)
plain	100	100	$4\frac{1}{2}$	$4\frac{1}{2}$	1 oz (30 g)
self-raising	95	95	$4\frac{1}{2}$	$4\frac{1}{2}$	1 oz (30 g)
wholemeal	90	90	$3\frac{1}{2}$	$3\frac{1}{2}$	1 oz (30 g)
frankfurters	80	80	$\frac{1}{4}$	$\frac{1}{4}$	1 small
French beans, boiled	2	10	0	0	5 oz (142 g)
French dressing	185	185	0	0	1 oz (30 ml)

	Calories per 1 oz (30 g)	Calories per portion	Carbohydrate units per 1 oz (30 g)	Carbohydrate units per portion	Size of average portion
fried bread	180	180	3	3	1 oz (30 g)
frogs' legs					
raw	20	20	0	0	1 oz (30 g)
fried in batter	85	255	0	0	12 legs

FRUIT & FRUIT JUICES

apples	10	60	$\frac{1}{2}$	$1\frac{1}{2}$	1 medium
chutney	55	55	3	3	1 oz (30 g)
cooking, raw	10	60	$\frac{1}{2}$	$1\frac{1}{2}$	1 medium
stewed, no sugar	10	50	$\frac{1}{2}$	$2\frac{1}{2}$	5 oz (142 g)
stewed + sugar	20	100	1	5	5 oz (142 g)
baked + sugar	10	60	$\frac{1}{2}$	$3\frac{1}{2}$	6 oz (171 g)
dried	65	65	$3\frac{1}{2}$	$3\frac{1}{2}$	1 oz (30 g)
juice, natural	15	65	$\frac{3}{4}$	$3\frac{1}{2}$	$\frac{1}{4}$ pt (142 ml)
sauce, no sugar	15	30	3	6	2 oz (57 g)
apricot					
fresh, raw	5	10	$\frac{1}{2}$	$\frac{1}{2}$	1 medium
stewed, no sugar	5	35	$\frac{1}{4}$	$1\frac{1}{2}$	5 oz (142 g)
stewed + sugar	15	85	1	$4\frac{1}{2}$	5 oz (142 g)
canned	30	120	$1\frac{1}{2}$	6	4 oz (114 g)
dried	50	50	$2\frac{1}{2}$	$2\frac{1}{2}$	1 oz (30 g)
stewed, no sugar	20	100	1	6	5 oz (142 g)
stewed + sugar	25	125	1	7	5 oz (142 g)
avocado pear	65	250	0	$\frac{1}{2}$	$\frac{1}{2}$ large

	Calories per 1 oz (30 g)	Calories per portion	Carbohydrate units per 1 oz (30 g)	Carbohydrate units per portion	Size of average portion
banana, weighed with skin	15	75	$\frac{3}{4}$	3	1 medium
bilberries, raw	15	65	$\frac{3}{4}$	3	4 oz (114 g)
blackberries					
raw	10	35	$\frac{1}{4}$	1	4 oz (114 g)
stewed, no sugar	5	30	$\frac{1}{4}$	1	4 oz (114 g)
stewed + sugar	15	65	$\frac{3}{4}$	$3\frac{1}{2}$	4 oz (114 g)
canned in syrup	15	65	$\frac{3}{4}$	$3\frac{1}{2}$	4 oz (114 g)
blackcurrants					
raw	10	35	$\frac{1}{4}$	1	4 oz (114 g)
stewed, no sugar	5	25	$\frac{1}{4}$	1	4 oz (114 g)
stewed + sugar	20	80	1	5	4 oz (114 g)
cherries					
eating, raw	10	45	$\frac{1}{2}$	2	4 oz (114 g)
cooking, raw	10	45	$\frac{1}{2}$	2	4 oz (114 g)
stewed, no sugar	10	45	$\frac{1}{2}$	2	4 oz (114 g)
stewed + sugar	20	80	1	4	4 oz (114 g)
canned	20	80	1	4	4 oz (114 g)
glacé	60	10	3	$\frac{1}{2}$	1 cherry
clementine	10	10	$\frac{1}{2}$	$\frac{1}{2}$	1 small
coconut, shelled, raw	100	100	$\frac{1}{4}$	$\frac{1}{4}$	1 oz (30 g)
cranberries, raw	4	4	$\frac{1}{4}$	$\frac{1}{4}$	1 oz (30 g)
damsons					
raw	10	40	$\frac{1}{2}$	2	4 oz (114 g)

	Calories per 1 oz (30 g)	Calories per portion	Carbohydrate units per 1 oz (30 g)	Carbohydrate units per portion	Size of average portion
stewed, no sugar	10	40	$\frac{1}{2}$	2	4 oz (114 g)
stewed + sugar	20	80	1	4	4 oz (114 g)
dates, dried	60	120	3	6	2 oz (57 g)
figs					
green, raw	10	15	$\frac{3}{4}$	1	1 fig
dried, raw	60	45	3	$2\frac{1}{2}$	1 fig
stewed, no sugar	35	170	$1\frac{1}{2}$	8	5 oz (142 g)
stewed + sugar	40	195	2	10	5 oz (142 g)
fruit salad, canned	25	110	$1\frac{1}{2}$	6	4 oz (114 g)
gooseberries					
green, raw	5	20	0	$\frac{3}{4}$	4 oz (114 g)
stewed, no sugar	4	15	0	$\frac{3}{4}$	4 oz (114 g)
stewed + sugar	15	55	$\frac{3}{4}$	3	4 oz (114 g)
ripe, raw	10	40	$\frac{1}{2}$	2	4 oz (114 g)
canned	40	120	2	8	4 oz (114 g)
grapefruit					
fresh	3	15	$\frac{1}{4}$	2	$\frac{1}{2}$ medium
canned	15	65	1	$3\frac{1}{2}$	4 oz (114 g)
juice, no sugar	10	50	$\frac{1}{2}$	2	$\frac{1}{4}$ pt (142 ml)
juice + sugar	10	55	$\frac{1}{2}$	3	$\frac{1}{4}$ pt (142 ml)
grapes					
black or white, raw	20	70	1	4	4 oz (114 g)
juice	20	100	1	9	$\frac{1}{4}$ pt (142 ml)
greengages					
raw	15	15	1	1	1 fruit

	Calories per 1 oz (30 g)	Calories per portion	Carbohydrate units per 1 oz (30 g)	Carbohydrate units per portion	Size of average portion
stewed, no sugar	10	45	$\frac{1}{2}$	2	4 oz (114 g)
stewed + sugar	20	85	1	4	4 oz (114 g)
guava, canned	15	60	1	4	4 oz (114 g)
lemon, whole	5	15	$\frac{1}{4}$	$\frac{1}{2}$	1 medium
lemon juice	2	2	0	0	1 oz (30 ml)
loganberries					
raw or stewed	5	20	$\frac{1}{4}$	1	4 oz (114 g)
stewed + sugar	15	60	$\frac{3}{4}$	3	4 oz (114 g)
canned	30	110	$1\frac{1}{2}$	6	4 oz (114 g)
lychees					
raw	20	20	1	1	1 oz (30 g)
canned	20	80	1	4	4 oz (114 g)
mandarin					
raw	10	25	$\frac{1}{2}$	1	1 medium
canned	15	60	1	4	4 oz (114 g)
mango					
raw	15	105	1	6	1 medium
canned	20	85	1	4	4 oz (114 g)
medlars, raw	10	10	$\frac{1}{2}$	$\frac{1}{2}$	1 large
melon					
cantaloupe	5	40	$\frac{1}{4}$	2	1 medium slice
honeydew	4	25	$\frac{1}{4}$	1	1 medium slice
ogen	3	20	$\frac{1}{4}$	1	$\frac{1}{2}$ medium

	Calories per 1 oz (30 g)	Calories per portion	Carbohydrate units per 1 oz (30 g)	Carbohydrate units per portion	Size of average portion
water	5	50	$\frac{1}{4}$	3	1 large slice
mulberries					
raw	10	40	$\frac{1}{2}$	2	4 oz (114 g)
canned	25	100	1	4	4 oz (114 g)
nectarines, raw	15	75	$\frac{3}{4}$	3	1 medium
oranges					
segments	10	40	$\frac{1}{2}$	2	4 oz (114 g)
whole	5	40	$\frac{1}{4}$	2	1 large
juice, fresh	10	50	$\frac{1}{2}$	$2\frac{1}{2}$	$\frac{1}{4}$ pt (142 ml)
canned, no sugar	10	100	$\frac{1}{2}$	5	$\frac{1}{4}$ pt (142 ml)
canned + sugar	15	75	$\frac{3}{4}$	$5\frac{1}{2}$	$\frac{1}{4}$ pt (142 ml)
passion fruit, raw	10	40	$\frac{1}{2}$	$1\frac{1}{2}$	4 oz (114 g)
paw-paw, canned	20	75	1	4	4 oz (114 g)
peaches					
fresh, raw	10	35	$\frac{1}{2}$	2	1 large
dried, raw	60	60	3	3	1 oz (30 g)
stewed, no sugar	20	90	1	4	4 oz (114 g)
stewed + sugar	25	105	$1\frac{1}{2}$	5	4 oz (114 g)
canned	25	100	$1\frac{1}{2}$	5	4 oz (114 g)
pears					
eating	10	45	$\frac{1}{2}$	2	1 small
cooking, raw	10	40	$\frac{1}{2}$	2	1 small
stewed, no sugar	10	35	$\frac{1}{2}$	2	4 oz (114 g)
stewed + sugar	20	75	1	4	4 oz (114 g)
canned	20	90	1	4	4 oz (114 g)

	Calories per 1 oz (30 g)	Calories per portion	Carbohydrate units per 1 oz (30 g)	Carbohydrate units per portion	Size of average portion
pineapple					
fresh	15	55	$\frac{3}{4}$	3	4 oz (114 g)
canned	20	90	1	4	4 oz (114 g)
juice, canned	15	75	$\frac{3}{4}$	4	$\frac{1}{4}$ pt (142 ml)
plums					
eating	10	10	$\frac{1}{2}$	$\frac{1}{2}$	1 medium
cooking, raw	5	25	$\frac{1}{2}$	1	4 oz (114 g)
stewed, no sugar	5	25	$\frac{1}{4}$	1	4 oz (114 g)
stewed + sugar	15	65	1	4	4 oz (114 g)
pomegranate					
raw	10	75	$\frac{3}{4}$	4	1 fruit
juice, no sugar	15	60	$\frac{1}{2}$	3	$\frac{1}{4}$ pt (142 ml)
prunes					
dried, raw	40	40	2	2	1 oz (30 g)
stewed, no sugar	25	95	1	4	4 oz (114 g)
stewed + sugar	30	120	$1\frac{1}{2}$	6	4 oz (114 g)
canned	25	100	$1\frac{1}{2}$	6	4 oz (114 g)
juice	20	110	1	5	$\frac{1}{4}$ pt (142 ml)
quince, raw	5	5	$\frac{1}{4}$	$\frac{1}{4}$	1 oz (30 g)
raisins, dried	70	70	$3\frac{1}{2}$	$3\frac{1}{2}$	1 oz (30 g)
raspberries					
raw	5	25	$\frac{1}{4}$	1	4 oz (114 g)
stewed, no sugar	5	25	$\frac{1}{4}$	1	4 oz (114 g)
stewed + sugar	20	80	1	4	4 oz (114 g)
canned	25	100	1	5	4 oz (114 g)

	Calories per 1 oz (30 g)	Calories per portion	Carbohydrate units per 1 oz (30 g)	Carbohydrate units per portion	Size of average portion
redcurrants					
raw	5	25	$\frac{1}{4}$	I	4 oz (114 g)
stewed, no sugar	5	20	$\frac{1}{4}$	I	4 oz (114 g)
stewed + sugar	15	60	$\frac{3}{4}$	3	4 oz (114 g)
rhubarb					
raw	2	10	0	0	5 oz (142 g)
stewed, no sugar	2	10	0	0	5 oz (142 g)
stewed + sugar	15	60	$\frac{3}{4}$	3	5 oz (142 g)
canned	15	75	$\frac{1}{2}$	3	5 oz (142 g)
satsuma	5	20	0	I	I medium
strawberries					
raw	10	45	$\frac{1}{4}$	2	6 oz (171 g)
canned	25	125	I	5	5 oz (142 g)
sultanas	70	70	$3\frac{1}{2}$	$3\frac{1}{2}$	1 oz (30 g)
tangerine	5	20	$\frac{1}{4}$	I	I medium
canned	15	60	I	3	4 oz (114 g)
white currants					
raw	5	30	$\frac{1}{4}$	I	4 oz (114 g)
stewed, no sugar	5	25	$\frac{1}{4}$	I	4 oz (114 g)
stewed + sugar	15	60	I	3	4 oz (114 g)
fruit cakes					
rich	95	280	3	9	3 oz (85 g)
iced	100	300	$3\frac{1}{2}$	10	3 oz (85 g)
plain	100	300	3	9	3 oz (85 g)
fruit gums	50	50	$2\frac{1}{2}$	$2\frac{1}{2}$	1 oz (30 g)

	Calories per 1 oz (30 g)	Calories per portion	Carbohydrate units per 1 oz (30 g)	Carbohydrate units per portion	Size of average portion
fruit salad, canned	25	110	$1\frac{1}{2}$	6	4 oz (114 g)
fruit shortcake biscuit	150	50	$4\frac{1}{2}$	$1\frac{1}{2}$	1 biscuit

garlic	5	1	0	0	1 clove
gelatine	95	15	0	0	1 tsp
ginger ale	10	30	$\frac{1}{2}$	2	4 oz (114 ml)
gingerbread	105	315	$3\frac{1}{2}$	10	3 oz (85 g)
gingernuts	130	65	$4\frac{1}{2}$	2	1 biscuit
glacé cherry	60	10	3	$\frac{1}{2}$	1 cherry
glucose	110	20	6	1	1 tsp
glucose drink	20	200	1	10	$\frac{1}{2}$ pt (284 ml)
golden syrup	85	85	$4\frac{1}{2}$	$4\frac{1}{2}$	1 tbsp
goose					
raw	65	65	0	0	1 oz (30 g)

	Calories per 1 oz (30 g)	Calories per portion	Carbohydrate units per 1 oz (30 g)	Carbohydrate units per portion	Size of average portion
roast	90	360	0	0	4 oz (114 g)
gooseberries					
green, raw	5	20	0	$\frac{3}{4}$	4 oz (114 g)
stewed, no sugar	4	15	0	$\frac{3}{4}$	4 oz (114 g)
stewed + sugar	15	55	$\frac{3}{4}$	3	4 oz (114 g)
ripe, raw	10	40	$\frac{1}{2}$	2	4 oz (114 g)
canned	40	120	2	8	4 oz (114 g)
grape juice	20	100	1	$4\frac{1}{2}$	$\frac{1}{4}$ pt (142 ml)
grapefruit					
fresh	3	15	$\frac{1}{4}$	2	$\frac{1}{2}$ medium
canned	15	65	1	$3\frac{1}{2}$	4 oz (114 g)
grapefruit juice					
no sugar	10	50	$\frac{1}{2}$	2	$\frac{1}{4}$ pt (142 ml)
+ sugar	10	55	$\frac{1}{2}$	3	$\frac{1}{4}$ pt (142 ml)
grapenuts	100	100	$4\frac{1}{2}$	$4\frac{1}{2}$	1 oz (30 g)
grapes					
black or white, raw	20	70	1	4	4 oz (114 g)
gravy browning powder	80	20	1	0	1 tsp
greengages					
raw	15	15	1	1	1 fruit
stewed, no sugar	10	45	$\frac{1}{2}$	2	4 oz (114 g)
stewed + sugar	20	85	1	4	4 oz (114 g)
grissini	85	15	$3\frac{1}{2}$	1	1 stick
grouse, roast	50	300	0	0	1 small

	Calories per 1 oz (30 g)	Calories per portion	Carbohydrate units per 1 oz (30 g)	Carbohydrate units per portion	Size of average portion
gruyère cheese	130	130	0	0	1 oz (30 g)
guava, canned	15	60	1	4	4 oz (114 g)

haddock					
fresh, raw	20	20	0	0	1 oz (30 g)
fresh, fried	50	250	0	0	5 oz (142 g)
fresh, steamed	30	150	0	0	5 oz (142 g)
smoked, raw	20	20	0	0	1 oz (30 g)
smoked, steamed	30	145	0	0	5 oz (142 g)
haggis boiled	90	525	1	6	6 oz (171 g)
hake					
raw	20	20	0	0	1 oz (30 g)
poached	30	150	0	0	5 oz (142 g)
halibut					
raw	25	25	0	0	1 oz (30 g)
steamed	35	185	0	0	5 oz (142 g)

	Calories per 1 oz (30 g)	Calories per portion	Carbohydrate units per 1 oz (30 g)	Carbohydrate units per portion	Size of average portion
poached	40	190	o	o	5 oz (142 g)
fried	50	240	o	o	5 oz (142 g)
ham					
boiled	75	230	o	o	3 oz (85 g)
smoked	60	190	o	o	3 oz (85 g)
canned	35	105	o	o	3 oz (85 g)
prosciutto	65	65	o	o	1 oz (30 g)
parma	65	65	o	o	1 oz (30 g)
ham & pork canned	75	230	o	o	3 oz (85 g)
hare					
raw	40	40	o	o	1 oz (30 g)
roast	55	215	o	o	4 oz (114 g)
stewed	55	320	o	o	6 oz (171 g)
haricot beans **boiled**	25	100	1	4	4 oz (114 g)
hazel nuts	110	110	$\frac{1}{4}$	$\frac{1}{4}$	1 oz (30 g)
heart					
lamb, raw	35	35	o	o	1 oz (30 g)
sheep, roast	65	270	o	o	4 oz (114 g)
ox, stewed	50	300	o	o	6 oz (171 g)
herring					
raw	65	65	o	o	1 oz (30 g)
steamed	55	280	o	o	5 oz (142 g)
fried in oatmeal	65	330	o	o	5 oz (142 g)
pickled	80	160	o	o	2 oz (57 g)

	Calories per 1 oz (30 g)	Calories per portion	Carbohydrate units per 1 oz (30 g)	Carbohydrate units per portion	Size of average portion
roe, fried	70	140	$\frac{1}{4}$	$\frac{1}{2}$	2 oz (57 g)
high protein corn flakes	110	55	$4\frac{1}{2}$	2	$\frac{1}{2}$ oz (14 g)
honey					
comb	80	160	4	8	2 oz (57 g)
in jars (clear & thick)	80	15	4	$\frac{3}{4}$	1 tsp
horseradish					
raw	15	15	$\frac{1}{2}$	$\frac{1}{2}$	1 oz (30 g)
sauce	60	30	$1\frac{1}{2}$	$\frac{3}{4}$	1 dsp
hot cross bun	80	310	$2\frac{1}{2}$	10	1 bun
hot pot	30	320	$\frac{1}{2}$	6	10 oz (284 g)
houmous	100	200	$\frac{1}{4}$	$\frac{1}{2}$	2 oz (57 g)
hovis bread	65	65	$2\frac{1}{2}$	$2\frac{1}{2}$	1 oz (30 g)

ice cream					
dairy, Cornish	45	95	$1\frac{1}{2}$	3	2 oz (57 g)
non-dairy	45	90	1	2	2 oz (57 g)

	Calories per 1 oz (30 g)	Calories per portion	Carbohydrate units per 1 oz (30 g)	Carbohydrate units per portion	Size of average portion
cassata	45	95	$1\frac{1}{2}$	3	2 oz (57 g)
chocolate	45	95	$1\frac{1}{2}$	3	2 oz (57 g)
pistachio	55	110	$1\frac{1}{2}$	3	2 oz (57 g)
strawberry	45	95	$1\frac{1}{2}$	3	2 oz (57 g)
ice cream cone	75	25	15	5	1 cone
ice cream wafer	75	10	15	3	1 wafer
instant porridge	110	110	4	4	1 oz (30 g)
instant whip	30	150	1	$4\frac{1}{2}$	5 oz (142 g)
Irish coffee	40	200	1	5	$\frac{1}{4}$ pt (142 ml)
Irish stew	35	530	$\frac{1}{2}$	9	15 oz (426 g)

jam all kinds	75	20	4	1	1 tsp
jam tart	120	120	$3\frac{1}{2}$	$3\frac{1}{2}$	1 tart
jellied eel	60	230	0	0	4 oz (114 g)
jellied veal	35	140	0	0	4 oz (114 g)

	Calories per 1 oz (30 g)	Calories per portion	Carbohydrate units per 1 oz (30 g)	Carbohydrate units per portion	Size of average portion
jelly					
made + water	15	70	$\frac{3}{4}$	3	4 oz (114 g)
made + milk	25	100	1	4	4 oz (114 g)
jelly cubes	75	75	$3\frac{1}{2}$	$3\frac{1}{2}$	1 oz (30 g)
Jerusalem artichokes, boiled	5	20	$\frac{1}{4}$	1	4 oz (114 g)

kedgeree	45	300	$\frac{1}{2}$	$3\frac{1}{2}$	7 oz (199 g)
keg bitter	10	100	$\frac{1}{2}$	5	$\frac{1}{2}$ pt (284 ml)
kidney					
lamb, raw	25	25	0	0	1 oz (30 g)
lamb, fried	45	180	0	0	4 oz (114 g)
ox, raw	25	25	0	0	1 oz (30 g)
ox, stewed	50	295	0	0	6 oz (171 g)
pig, raw	25	25	0	0	1 oz (30 g)
pig, stewed	45	260	0	0	6 oz (171 g)

	Calories per 1 oz (30 g)	Calories per portion	Carbohydrate units per 1 oz (30 g)	Carbohydrate units per portion	Size of average portion
kipper					
raw	80	80	0	0	1 oz (30 g)
baked	60	290	0	0	5 oz (142 g)
fried	70	340	0	0	5 oz (142 g)
kirsch	65	65	3	3	1 oz (30 ml)
kohlrabi					
raw	5	5	0	0	1 oz (30 ml)
boiled	3	15	0	0	5 oz (142 g)

ladies' fingers					
raw	5	5	0	0	1 oz (30 g)
boiled	5	20	0	$\frac{1}{2}$	4 oz (114 g)
canned	5	20	0	$\frac{1}{2}$	4 oz (114 g)

	Calories per 1 oz (30 g)	Calories per portion	Carbohydrate units per 1 oz (30 g)	Carbohydrate units per portion	Size of average portion
lager					
bottled	10	100	$\frac{1}{2}$	3	$\frac{1}{2}$ pt (284 ml)
draught	10	100	$\frac{1}{2}$	3	$\frac{1}{2}$ pt (284 ml)
lamb					
lean, raw	45	45	0	0	1 oz (30 g)
fat, raw	190	190	0	0	1 oz (30 g)
breast, raw	110	110	0	0	1 oz (30 g)
breast, roast	115	470	0	0	4 oz (114 g)
chop, raw	105	105	0	0	1 oz (30 g)
chop, grilled	100	400	0	0	4 oz (114 g)
cutlet, raw	110	110	0	0	1 oz (30 g)
cutlet, grilled	105	210	0	0	1 cutlet
leg, raw	70	70	0	0	1 oz (30 g)
leg, roast	75	300	0	0	4 oz (114 g)
scrag & neck, raw	90	90	0	0	1 oz (30 g)
scrag & neck, stewed	85	345	0	0	5 oz (142 g)
shoulder, raw	90	90	0	0	1 oz (30 g)
shoulder, roast	90	360	0	0	4 oz (114 g)
lancashire cheese	100	100	0	0	1 oz (30 g)
lard	255	255	0	0	1 oz (30 g)
lardy cake	105	410	$3\frac{1}{2}$	$14\frac{1}{2}$	4 oz (114 g)
laverbread	15	15	0	0	1 oz (30 g)
leeks					
raw	10	10	0	0	1 oz (30 g)
boiled	5	30	0	0	4 oz (114 g)

	Calories per 1 oz (30 g)	Calories per portion	Carbohydrate units per 1 oz (30 g)	Carbohydrate units per portion	Size of average portion
leicester cheese	110	110	0	0	1 oz (30 g)
lemons whole	5	15	$\frac{1}{4}$	$\frac{1}{2}$	1 medium
lemon curd	80	15	$3\frac{1}{2}$	$\frac{1}{2}$	1 tsp
homemade	80	15	2	$\frac{1}{4}$	1 tsp
lemon juice fresh	2	2	0	0	1 oz (30 ml)
lemon meringue pie	90	370	$2\frac{1}{2}$	10	4 oz (114 g)
lemon mousse frozen	40	110	1	$2\frac{1}{2}$	$3\frac{1}{2}$ oz (100 g)
lemon sole					
raw	25	25	0	0	1 oz (30 g)
steamed	25	130	0	0	5 oz (142 g)
fried in breadcrumbs	60	310	0	$\frac{1}{2}$	5 oz (142 g)
lemon sponge	145	170	$5\frac{1}{2}$	6	1 small slice
lemon squash, undiluted	30	30	$1\frac{1}{2}$	$1\frac{1}{2}$	1 oz (30 ml)
lemonade, bottled	5	60	$\frac{1}{4}$	3	$\frac{1}{2}$ pt (284 ml)
lentils					
raw	85	85	3	3	1 oz (30 g)
split or whole, boiled	30	120	1	4	4 oz (114 g)
dahl masur	25	105	$\frac{3}{4}$	$1\frac{1}{2}$	4 oz (114 g)
lentil soup	30	300	$\frac{3}{4}$	6	$\frac{1}{2}$ pt (284 ml)
lettuce raw	3	10	0	0	3 oz (85 g)
lime juice, undiluted	30	30	$1\frac{1}{2}$	$1\frac{1}{2}$	1 oz (30 ml)

	Calories per 1 oz (30 g)	Calories per portion	Carbohydrate units per 1 oz (30 g)	Carbohydrate units per portion	Size of average portion
liquorice all sorts	90	350	4	16	4 oz (114 g)
liver					
calf, raw	45	45	0	0	1 oz (30 g)
calf, fried	70	290	0	0	4 oz (114 g)
chicken, raw	40	40	0	0	1 oz (30 g)
chicken, fried	55	220	0	1	4 oz (114 g)
lamb, raw	50	50	0	0	1 oz (30 g)
lamb, fried	65	260	$\frac{1}{4}$	1	4 oz (114 g)
ox, raw	45	45	0	0	1 oz (30 g)
ox, stewed	55	335	$\frac{1}{4}$	1	6 oz (171 g)
pig, raw	45	45	0	0	1 oz (30 g)
pig, stewed	55	320	$\frac{1}{4}$	1	6 oz (171 g)
liver sausage	90	180	$\frac{1}{4}$	$\frac{1}{2}$	2 oz (57 g)
lobster boiled	35	175	0	0	5 oz (142 g)
loganberries					
raw	5	20	$\frac{1}{4}$	1	4 oz (114 g)
stewed, no sugar	5	20	$\frac{1}{4}$	1	4 oz (114 g)
stewed + sugar	15	60	$\frac{3}{4}$	3	4 oz (114 g)
canned	30	110	$1\frac{1}{2}$	6	4 oz (114 g)
low fat spread	105	20	0	0	1 tsp
luncheon meat, canned	90	270	$\frac{1}{4}$	1	3 oz (85 g)
lychee					
raw	20	20	1	1	1 oz (30 g)
canned	20	80	1	4	4 oz (114 g)

	Calories per 1 oz (30 g)	Calories per portion	Carbohydrate units per 1 oz (30 g)	Carbohydrate units per portion	Size of average portion
macaroni					
raw	105	105	$4\frac{1}{2}$	$4\frac{1}{2}$	1 oz (30 g)
boiled	35	350	$1\frac{1}{2}$	14	10 oz (284 g)
macaroni cheese	50	500	1	10	10 oz (284 g)
macaroon	100	200	$2\frac{1}{2}$	5	1 large
mackerel					
raw	65	65	0	0	1 oz (30 g)
fried	55	275	0	0	5 oz (142 g)
steamed	75	380	0	0	5 oz (142 g)
smoked	90	440	0	0	5 oz (142 g)
madeira	35	35	$1\frac{1}{2}$	$1\frac{1}{2}$	1 oz (30 ml)
madeira cake	110	330	$3\frac{1}{2}$	10	3 oz (85 g)
maize oil	255	255	0	0	1 oz (30 ml)
malt bread	70	70	3	3	1 oz (30 g)
malted milk powder	115	40	4	1	2 tsp

	Calories per 1 oz (30 g)	Calories per portion	Carbohydrate units per 1 oz (30 g)	Carbohydrate units per portion	Size of average portion
mandarin					
raw	10	25	$\frac{1}{2}$	1	1 small
canned	15	160	1	4	4 oz (114 g)
mango					
raw	15	105	1	6	1 medium
canned	20	85	1	4	4 oz (114 g)
margarine	210	50	0	0	1 tsp
marmalade	75	20	4	1	1 tsp
marrow					
raw	3	3	0	0	1 oz (30 g)
boiled	1	5	0	0	4 oz (114 g)
marshmallow	95	95	$4\frac{1}{2}$	$4\frac{1}{2}$	1 oz (30 g)
marzipan	125	125	3	3	1 oz (30 g)
matzo biscuit	110	110	5	5	1 oz (30 g)
mayonnaise, homemade	205	100	0	0	1 dsp

MEAT

bacon

gammon joint

raw	65	65	0	0	1 oz (30 g)
boiled	75	300	0	0	4 oz (114 g)
gammon rashers, grilled	65	260	0	0	4 oz (114 g)

	Calories per 1 oz (30 g)	Calories per portion	Carbohydrate units per 1 oz (30 g)	Carbohydrate units per portion	Size of average portion
rashers, raw					
back	120	360	0	0	2 rashers
middle	120	360	0	0	2 rashers
streaky	120	240	0	0	2 rashers
rashers, fried					
back	130	260	0	0	2 rashers
middle	135	270	0	0	2 rashers
streaky	140	210	0	0	2 rashers
rashers, grilled					
back	115	160	0	0	2 rashers
middle	120	190	0	0	2 rashers
streaky	120	130	0	0	2 rashers
beef					
lean, raw	35	35	0	0	1 oz (30 g)
fat, raw	180	180	0	0	1 oz (30 g)
brisket, boiled	90	380	0	0	4 oz (114 g)
forerib, roast	100	400	0	0	4 oz (114 g)
steak					
raw	55	55	0	0	1 oz (30 g)
grilled	55	330	0	0	6 oz (171 g) weighed raw
fried	65	390	0	0	6 oz (171 g) weighed raw
joint, roast	100	400	0	0	4 oz (114 g)
corned	60	120	0	0	2 oz (57 g)

	Calories per 1 oz (30 g)	Calories per portion	Carbohydrate units per 1 oz (30 g)	Carbohydrate units per portion	Size of average portion
minced					
lean, raw	35	35	o	o	1 oz (30 g)
fat, raw	65	65	o	o	1 oz (30 g)
stewed	65	260	o	o	4 oz (114 g)
silverside					
boiled	70	280	o	o	4 oz (114 g)
boiled, lean only	50	200	o	o	4 oz (114 g)
sirloin roast	80	240	o	o	3 oz (85 g)
stewing steak					
raw	50	50	o	o	1 oz (30 g)
stewed	65	260	o	o	4 oz (114 g)
frogs' legs					
raw	20	20	o	o	1 oz (30 g)
fried in batter	85	255	o	o	12 legs
lamb					
lean, raw	45	45	o	o	1 oz (30 g)
fat, raw	190	190	o	o	1 oz (30 g)
breast, raw	110	110	o	o	1 oz (30 g)
breast, roast	115	470	o	o	4 oz (114 g)
chop, raw	105	105	o	o	1 oz (30 g)
chop, grilled	100	400	o	o	4 oz (114 g)
cutlet, raw	110	110	o	o	1 oz (30 g)
cutlet, grilled	105	210	o	o	4 oz (114 g)
leg, raw	70	70	o	o	1 oz (30 g)
leg roast	75	300	o	o	4 oz (114 g)

	Calories per 1 oz (30 g)	Calories per portion	Carbohydrate units per 1 oz (30 g)	Carbohydrate units per portion	Size of average portion
scrag & neck, raw	90	90	0	0	1 oz (30 g)
scrag & neck, stewed	85	345	0	0	5 oz (142 g)
shoulder, raw	90	90	0	0	1 oz (30 g)
shoulder, roast	90	360	0	0	4 oz (114 g)
pork					
lean, raw	40	40	0	0	1 oz (30 g)
fat, raw	190	190	0	0	1 oz (30 g)
belly rashers, raw	110	110	0	0	1 oz (30 g)
belly rashers, grilled	115	450	0	0	4 oz (114 g)
chop, raw	95	95	0	0	1 oz (30 g)
chop, grilled	95	565	0	0	1 chop
ham					
boiled	75	230	0	0	3 oz (85 g)
smoked	60	190	0	0	3 oz (85 g)
canned	35	105	0	0	3 oz (85 g)
prosciutto	65	65	0	0	1 oz (30 g)
parma	65	65	0	0	1 oz (30 g)
leg, raw	75	75	0	0	1 oz (30 g)
leg, roast	80	325	0	0	4 oz (114 g)
snails with butter	180	270	0	0	6 snails
veal					
cutlet, fried	60	365	$\frac{1}{4}$	$1\frac{1}{2}$	1 cutlet
fillet, raw	30	30	0	0	1 oz (30 g)
fillet, roast	65	260	0	0	4 oz (114 g)
jellied	35	140	0	0	4 oz (114 g)

	Calories per 1 oz (30 g)	Calories per portion	Carbohydrate units per 1 oz (30 g)	Carbohydrate units per portion	Size of average portion
MEAT PRODUCTS					
beefburgers					
fried	75	300	0	0	1 average
grilled	75	290	0	1	1 average
beef steak pudding	65	390	1	6	6 oz (171 g)
beef stew	35	210	$\frac{1}{4}$	1	6 oz (171 g)
black pudding	85	170	1	2	2 oz (57 g)
bolognese sauce	40	240	$\frac{1}{4}$	1	6 oz (171 g)
brawn	45	90	0	0	2 oz (57 g)
cornish pasty	95	570	2	11	6 oz (171 g)
curried meat	45	270	$\frac{1}{2}$	$2\frac{1}{2}$	6 oz (171 g)
faggots	75	600	$\frac{3}{4}$	7	2 faggots
frankfurters	80	80	$\frac{1}{4}$	$\frac{1}{4}$	1 small
haggis boiled	90	525	0	0	6 oz (171 g)
hot pot	30	320	$\frac{1}{2}$	6	10 oz (284 g)
Irish stew	35	530	$\frac{1}{2}$	9	15 oz (426 g)
luncheon meat canned	90	270	$\frac{1}{4}$	1	3 oz (85 g)
meat paste	50	10	0	0	1 tsp
mortadella	85	285	0	0	3 oz (85 g)
moussaka	55	550	$\frac{1}{2}$	5	10 oz (284 g)
pâté (chicken liver, duck & game)	95	95	0	0	1 oz (30 g)
pâté, goose liver	110	110	0	0	1 oz (30 g)
polony	80	160	1	2	2 oz (57 g)

	Calories per 1 oz (30 g)	Calories per portion	Carbohydrate units per 1 oz (30 g)	Carbohydrate units per portion	Size of average portion
salami	140	280	0	0	2 oz (57 g)
sausages					
beef, fried	75	150	$\frac{1}{2}$	1	1 sausage
beef, grilled	55	110	$\frac{1}{2}$	1	1 sausage
pork, fried	90	180	$\frac{1}{2}$	1	1 sausage
pork, grilled	90	125	$\frac{3}{4}$	1	1 sausage
sausage roll					
flaky pastry	135	270	2	4	1 small
short pastry	110	220	2	4	1 small
saveloy	75	150	$\frac{1}{2}$	1	2 oz (57 g)
shepherd's pie	35	350	$\frac{1}{2}$	5	10 oz (284 g)
steak & kidney pie					
single crust	80	640	1	8	8 oz (227 g)
individual	90	735	$1\frac{1}{2}$	11	8 oz (227 g)
stewed steak with gravy	50	400	0	0	8 oz (227 g)
white pudding	130	255	2	4	2 oz (57 g)
medlars, raw	10	10	$\frac{1}{2}$	$\frac{1}{2}$	1 large
melons					
cantaloupe	5	40	$\frac{1}{4}$	2	1 medium slice
honeydew	4	25	$\frac{1}{4}$	1	1 medium slice
ogen	3	20	$\frac{1}{4}$	1	$\frac{1}{2}$ medium
water	5	50	$\frac{1}{4}$	3	1 large slice

	Calories per 1 oz (30 g)	Calories per portion	Carbohydrate units per 1 oz (30 g)	Carbohydrate units per portion	Size of average portion
meringue	110	50	$5\frac{1}{2}$	$2\frac{1}{2}$	1 large
milk, cows					
whole	20	20	$\frac{1}{4}$	$\frac{1}{4}$	1 oz (30 ml)
sterilized	20	20	$\frac{1}{4}$	$\frac{1}{4}$	1 oz (30 ml)
long life	20	20	$\frac{1}{4}$	$\frac{1}{4}$	1 oz (30 ml)
skimmed	10	10	$\frac{1}{4}$	$\frac{1}{4}$	1 oz (30 ml)
semi-skimmed (light)	15	15	$\frac{1}{4}$	$\frac{1}{4}$	1 oz (30 ml)
condensed, whole, sweetened	90	90	3	3	1 oz (30 ml)
skimmed, sweetened	75	75	$3\frac{1}{2}$	$3\frac{1}{2}$	1 oz (30 ml)
evaporated, whole, unsweetened	45	45	$\frac{3}{4}$	$\frac{3}{4}$	1 oz (30 ml)
dried, whole	140	35	2	$\frac{1}{2}$	2 tsp
dried, skimmed	100	15	3	$\frac{1}{2}$	2 tsp
milk, goats	20	20	$\frac{1}{4}$	$\frac{1}{4}$	1 oz (30 ml)
milk jelly	25	100	1	4	4 oz (114 g)
milk pudding	35	220	1	6	6 oz (171 g)
canned rice	25	150	$\frac{3}{4}$	5	6 oz (171 g)
mince pies	125	210	$3\frac{1}{2}$	6	1 pie
mincemeat	65	65	$3\frac{1}{2}$	$3\frac{1}{2}$	1 oz (30 g)
minerals					
bitter lemon	10	40	$\frac{1}{2}$	2	4 oz (114 ml)
ginger ale	10	30	$\frac{1}{2}$	2	4 oz (114 ml)
soda water	0	0	0	0	4 oz (114 ml)
tonic water	5	20	$\frac{1}{4}$	1	4 oz (114 ml)

	Calories per 1 oz (30 g)	Calories per portion	Carbohydrate units per 1 oz (30 g)	Carbohydrate units per portion	Size of average portion
minestrone soup	5	65	$\frac{1}{4}$	2	$\frac{1}{2}$ pt (284 ml)
mint sauce (in jars, undiluted)	30	30	$1\frac{1}{2}$	$1\frac{1}{2}$	1 oz (30 g)
mortadella	85	285	0	0	3 oz (85 g)
moussaka	55	550	$\frac{1}{2}$	5	10 oz (284 g)
mousse, frozen					
chocolate	35	100	1	3	$3\frac{1}{2}$ oz (100 g)
fruit	40	110	1	$2\frac{1}{2}$	$3\frac{1}{2}$ oz (100 g)
mozzarella cheese	95	95	0	0	1 oz (30 g)
muesli	105	210	4	8	2 oz (57 g)
muffin	65	130	3	$5\frac{1}{2}$	1 muffin
mulberries					
raw	10	40	$\frac{1}{2}$	2	4 oz (114 g)
canned	25	100	1	4	4 oz (114 g)
mullet					
raw	40	40	0	0	1 oz (30 g)
steamed	50	250	0	0	5 oz (142 g)
fried	60	300	0	0	5 oz (142 g)
mulligatawny soup	10	100	$\frac{1}{2}$	3	$\frac{1}{2}$ pt (284 ml)
mung beans					
raw	65	65	2	2	1 oz (30 g)
cooked dahl	30	60	$\frac{3}{4}$	$1\frac{1}{2}$	2 oz (57 g)
mushrooms					
raw	4	4	0	0	1 oz (30 g)
boiled	2	5	0	0	2 oz (57 g)

	Calories per 1 oz (30 g)	Calories per portion	Carbohydrate units per 1 oz (30 g)	Carbohydrate units per portion	Size of average portion
fried	60	120	0	0	2 oz (57 g)
mushroom soup **canned**	15	150	$\frac{1}{4}$	2	$\frac{1}{2}$ pt (284 ml)
mussels					
raw	20	20	0	0	1 oz (30 g)
steamed	25	75	0	0	3 oz (85 g)
canned	20	55	0	0	3 oz (85 g)
mustard powder	130	15	1	0	1 tsp
mustard & cress	3	3	0	0	1 oz (30 g)

nectarines, raw	15	45	$\frac{3}{4}$	2	1 medium

NUTS

almonds	160	320	$\frac{1}{4}$	$\frac{1}{2}$	2 oz (57 g)
Brazil nuts	175	350	$\frac{1}{4}$	$\frac{1}{2}$	2 oz (57 g)

	Calories per 1 oz (30 g)	Calories per portion	Carbohydrate units per 1 oz (30 g)	Carbohydrate units per portion	Size of average portion
cashew nuts	155	610	1	$3\frac{1}{2}$	4 oz (114 g)
chestnuts	50	100	2	4	2 oz (57 g)
hazelnuts	110	110	$\frac{1}{4}$	$\frac{1}{4}$	1 oz (30 g)
peanuts, fresh or dry roasted or roasted and salted	160	160	$\frac{1}{2}$	$\frac{1}{2}$	1 oz (30 g)
pistachio nuts, shelled, raw	170	170	1	1	1 oz (30 g)
walnuts, shelled	150	150	$\frac{1}{4}$	$\frac{1}{4}$	1 oz (30 g)

oatcakes	125	60	$3\frac{1}{2}$	2	1 biscuit
oatmeal, raw	115	115	4	4	1 oz (30 g)
octopus					
raw	20	20	0	0	1 oz (30 g)
steamed	25	125	0	0	5 oz (142 g)

	Calories per 1 oz (30 g)	Calories per portion	Carbohydrate units per 1 oz (30 g)	Carbohydrate units per portion	Size of average portion
fried	30	160	0	0	5 oz (142 g)
fried in batter	55	340	$\frac{1}{2}$	$2\frac{1}{2}$	5 oz (142 g)

OFFAL

brain
calf, boiled	45	135	0	0	3 oz (85 g)
lamb, boiled	35	105	0	0	3 oz (85 g)

heart
lamb, raw	35	35	0	0	1 oz (30 g)
sheep, roast	65	270	0	0	4 oz (114 g)
ox, raw	30	30	0	0	1 oz (30 g)
ox, stewed	50	300	0	0	6 oz (171 g)

kidney
lamb, raw	25	25	0	0	1 oz (30 g)
lamb, fried	45	180	0	0	4 oz (114 g)
ox, raw	25	25	0	0	1 oz (30 g)
ox, stewed	50	295	0	0	6 oz (171 g)
pig, raw	25	25	0	0	1 oz (30 g)
pig, stewed	45	260	0	0	6 oz (171 g)

liver
calf, raw	45	45	0	0	1 oz (30 g)
calf, fried	70	290	0	0	4 oz (114 g)
chicken, raw	40	40	0	0	1 oz (30 g)
chicken, fried	55	220	0	1	4 oz (114 g)

	Calories per 1 oz (30 g)	Calories per portion	Carbohydrate units per 1 oz (30 g)	Carbohydrate units per portion	Size of average portion
lamb, raw	50	50	0	0	1 oz (30 g)
lamb, fried	65	260	$\frac{1}{4}$	1	4 oz (114 g)
ox, raw	45	45	0	0	1 oz (30 g)
ox, stewed	55	335	$\frac{1}{4}$	1	6 oz (171 g)
pig, raw	45	45	0	0	1 oz (30 g)
pig, stewed	55	320	$\frac{1}{4}$	1	6 oz (171 g)
oxtail					
raw	50	50	0	0	1 oz (30 g)
stewed	70	515	$\frac{1}{4}$	2	8 oz (227 g)
sweetbread					
lamb, raw	35	35	0	0	1 oz (30 g)
lamb, fried	65	260	$\frac{1}{4}$	1	4 oz (114 g)
tongue					
lamb, raw	55	55	0	0	1 oz (30 g)
sheep, stewed	80	490	0	0	6 oz (171 g)
ox, pickled	60	60	0	0	1 oz (30 g)
ox, pickled and boiled	85	170	0	0	2 oz (57 g)
canned	60	120	0	0	2 oz (57 g)
tripe					
dressed	15	15	0	0	1 oz (30 g)
stewed	30	180	0	0	6 oz (171 g)
okra					
raw	5	5	0	0	1 oz (30 g)
boiled	5	20	0	0	4 oz (114 g)
canned	5	20	0	0	4 oz (114 g)

	Calories per 1 oz (30 g)	Calories per portion	Carbohydrate units per 1 oz (30 g)	Carbohydrate units per portion	Size of average portion
olives					
black or green	25	25	0	0	10 olives
stuffed	30	30	0	0	10 olives
olive oil	255	255	0	0	1 oz (30 ml)
omelette, plain	55	275	0	0	5 oz (142 g)
onions					
raw	5	5	0	0	1 oz (30 g)
boiled	4	15	0	0	4 oz (114 g)
fried	100	100	$\frac{1}{2}$	$\frac{1}{2}$	1 oz (30 g)
pickled	5	5	0	0	1 oz (30 g)
spring, raw	10	3	0	0	1 onion
onion sauce	30	90	$\frac{1}{2}$	$1\frac{1}{2}$	3 oz (85 g)
oranges					
segments	10	40	$\frac{1}{2}$	2	4 oz (114 g)
whole	5	40	$\frac{1}{4}$	2	1 large
orange juice fresh or canned, no sugar	10	50	$\frac{1}{2}$	$2\frac{1}{2}$	$\frac{1}{4}$ pt (142 ml)
canned + sugar	15	75	$\frac{3}{4}$	$5\frac{1}{2}$	$\frac{1}{4}$ pt (142 ml)
orange marmalade	75	20	4	1	1 tsp
orange squash, undiluted	30	30	$1\frac{1}{2}$	$1\frac{1}{2}$	1 oz (30 ml)
ouzo	65	65	3	3	1 oz (30 ml)
oxtail					
raw	50	50	0	0	1 oz (30 g)

	Calories per 1 oz (30 g)	Calories per portion	Carbohydrate units per 1 oz (30 g)	Carbohydrate units per portion	Size of average portion
stewed	70	515	$\frac{1}{4}$	2	8 oz (227 g)
oxtail soup	15	150	0	2	$\frac{1}{2}$ pt (284 ml)
oysters					
raw	15	15	0	0	2 oysters
canned	15	45	0	0	6 oysters
smoked	15	45	0	0	3 oz (85 g)

pale ale, bottled	10	100	$\frac{1}{2}$	5	$\frac{1}{2}$ pt (284 ml)
palm heart, canned	30	120	$1\frac{1}{2}$	6	4 oz (114 g)
palm oil	255	255	0	0	1 oz (30 ml)
palmier	160	55	3	1	1 biscuit
pancakes	85	85	2	2	1 thin.

	Calories per 1 oz (30 g)	Calories per portion	Carbohydrate units per 1 oz (30 g)	Carbohydrate units per portion	Size of average portion
parma ham	65	65	0	0	1 oz (30 g)
parmesan cheese	120	20	0	0	2 tsp
parsley, raw	5	5	0	0	1 oz (30 g)
parsnips, boiled	15	60	$\frac{3}{4}$	3	4 oz (114 g)
partridge, roast	60	240	0	0	4 oz (114 g)
passion fruit, raw	10	40	$\frac{1}{2}$	$1\frac{1}{2}$	4 oz (114 g)
pasty, Cornish	95	570	2	11	6 oz (171 g)
pastis	70	70	3	3	1 oz (30 ml)
pastilles, fruit	70	70	$3\frac{1}{2}$	$3\frac{1}{2}$	1 oz (30 g)
pastry, choux					
raw	60	60	1	1	1 oz (30 g)
cooked	95	95	$1\frac{1}{2}$	$1\frac{1}{2}$	1 oz (30 g)
pastry, flaky					
raw	120	120	2	2	1 oz (30 g)
cooked	160	160	$2\frac{1}{2}$	$2\frac{1}{2}$	1 oz (30 g)
pastry, short					
raw	130	130	$2\frac{1}{2}$	$2\frac{1}{2}$	1 oz (30 g)
cooked	150	150	3	3	1 oz (30 g)
pâté, chicken liver, duck & game	95	95	0	0	1 oz (30 g)
pâté, goose liver	110	110	0	0	1 oz (30 g)
paw-paw, canned	20	75	1	4	4 oz (114 g)
peaches					
fresh, raw	10	35	$\frac{1}{2}$	2	1 large
dried, raw	60	60	3	3	1 oz (30 g)

	Calories per 1 oz (30 g)	Calories per portion	Carbohydrate units per 1 oz (30 g)	Carbohydrate units per portion	Size of average portion
stewed, no sugar	10	35	$\frac{1}{2}$	2	4 oz (114 g)
stewed + sugar	20	75	1	4	4 oz (114 g)
canned	20	90	1	4	4 oz (114 g)
peach jam	75	20	4	1	1 tsp
peanuts, fresh or dry roasted & salted	160	160	$\frac{1}{2}$	$\frac{1}{2}$	1 oz (30 g)
peanut brittle	120	120	4	4	1 oz (30 g)
peanut butter	175	175	$\frac{3}{4}$	$\frac{3}{4}$	1 oz (30 g)
peanut oil	255	255	0	0	1 oz (30 ml)
pears					
eating	10	45	$\frac{1}{2}$	2	1 small
cooking, raw	10	40	$\frac{1}{2}$	2	1 small
stewed, no sugar	10	35	$\frac{1}{2}$	2	4 oz (114 g)
stewed + sugar	20	75	1	4	4 oz (114 g)
canned	20	90	1	4	4 oz (114 g)
pears, avocado	65	250	0	$\frac{1}{2}$	$\frac{1}{2}$ large
pearl barley					
raw	100	100	5	5	1 oz (30 g)
boiled	35	35	2	2	1 oz (30 g)
peas					
fresh, raw	20	20	$\frac{1}{2}$	$\frac{1}{2}$	1 oz (30 g)
fresh, boiled	15	45	$\frac{1}{2}$	1	3 oz (85 g)
frozen, raw	15	15	$\frac{1}{2}$	$\frac{1}{2}$	1 oz (30 g)
frozen, boiled	10	30	$\frac{1}{4}$	1	3 oz (85 g)
canned, garden	15	45	$\frac{1}{2}$	1	3 oz (85 g)

	Calories per 1 oz (30 g)	Calories per portion	Carbohydrate units per 1 oz (30 g)	Carbohydrate units per portion	Size of average portion
canned, processed	25	65	$\frac{3}{4}$	3	3 oz (85 g)
dried, raw	80	80	3	3	1 oz (30 g)
dried, boiled	30	90	1	3	3 oz (85 g)
split, raw	90	90	3	3	1 oz (30 g)
split, boiled	35	105	1	4	3 oz (85 g)
chick, raw	90	90	3	3	1 oz (30 g)
chick, cooked dahl	40	160	1	4	4 oz (114 g)
red pigeon, raw	85	85	3	3	1 oz (30 g)
red pigeon, cooked	30	90	1	3	3 oz (85 g)
peppers					
raw	4	10	0	0	2 oz (57 g)
boiled	4	10	0	0	2 oz (57 g)
peppermint creams, chocolate coated	120	120	4	4	1 oz (30 g)
peppermints	110	110	6	6	1 oz (30 g)
pheasant, roast	60	240	0	0	4 oz (114 g)
piccalilli	10	10	$\frac{1}{4}$	$\frac{1}{4}$	1 oz (30 g)
pickle, sweet	40	40	2	2	1 oz (30 g)
pickled onions	5	5	0	0	1 oz (30 g)
pie					
apple	50	300	$1\frac{1}{2}$	$7\frac{1}{2}$	6 oz (171 g)
fish	35	280	$\frac{1}{4}$	6	8 oz (227 g)
gooseberry	50	300	$1\frac{1}{2}$	$7\frac{1}{2}$	6 oz (171 g)
lemon meringue	90	370	$2\frac{1}{2}$	10	4 oz (114 g)
mince	125	210	$3\frac{1}{2}$	6	1 pie

	Calories per 1 oz (30 g)	Calories per portion	Carbohydrate units per 1 oz (30 g)	Carbohydrate units per portion	Size of average portion
plum	50	300	$1\frac{1}{2}$	$7\frac{1}{2}$	6 oz (171 g)
pork	105	420	$1\frac{1}{2}$	6	4 oz (114 g)
rhubarb	50	300	$1\frac{1}{2}$	$7\frac{1}{2}$	6 oz (171 g)
shepherd's	35	350	$\frac{1}{2}$	5	10 oz (284 g)
pigeon, roast	65	260	0	0	4 oz (114 g)
pigeon peas					
raw	85	85	3	3	1 oz (30 g)
cooked	30	90	1	3	3 oz (85 g)
pilchards					
canned in oil	65	250	0	0	4 oz (114 g)
canned in tomato sauce	35	140	0	$\frac{1}{4}$	4 oz (114 g)
pineapple					
fresh	15	55	$\frac{3}{4}$	3	4 oz (114 g)
canned	20	90	1	4	4 oz (114 g)
juice, canned	15	75	$\frac{3}{4}$	4	$\frac{1}{4}$ pt (142 ml)
pistachio nuts, shelled raw	170	170	1	1	1 oz (30 g)
pizza, cheese & tomato	65	260	$1\frac{1}{2}$	6	1 small
plaice					
raw	25	25	0	0	1 oz (30 g)
steamed	25	130	0	0	5 oz (142 g)
fried in batter	80	400	$\frac{3}{4}$	4	5 oz (142 g)
fried in breadcrumbs	65	325	$\frac{1}{2}$	$2\frac{1}{2}$	5 oz (142 g)

	Calories per 1 oz (30 g)	Calories per portion	Carbohydrate units per 1 oz (30 g)	Carbohydrate units per portion	Size of average portion
plantain					
green, boiled	35	140	2	7	4 oz (114 g)
ripe, fried	75	300	$2\frac{1}{2}$	7	4 oz (114 g)
plums					
fresh, raw	10	10	$\frac{1}{2}$	$\frac{1}{2}$	1 medium
cooking, raw	5	25	$\frac{1}{2}$	1	4 oz (114 g)
stewed, no sugar	5	25	$\frac{1}{4}$	1	4 oz (114 g)
stewed + sugar	15	65	1	4	4 oz (114 g)
plum jam	75	20	4	1	1 tsp
plum pie	50	300	$1\frac{1}{2}$	$7\frac{1}{2}$	6 oz (171 g)
polony	80	160	1	2	2 oz (57 g)
pomegranate					
raw	10	75	$\frac{3}{4}$	4	1 fruit
juice, no sugar	15	60	$\frac{1}{2}$	3	$\frac{1}{4}$ pt (142 ml)
popadom, grilled	100	100	4	4	3 popadoms
popcorn					
plain	110	110	4	4	1 oz (30 g)
+ oil & salt	130	130	3	3	1 oz (30 g)
+ sugar	110	110	5	5	1 oz (30 g)
pork					
lean, raw	40	40	0	0	1 oz (30 g)
fat, raw	190	190	0	0	1 oz (30 g)
belly rashers, raw	110	110	0	0	1 oz (30 g)
belly rashers, grilled	115	450	0	0	4 oz (114 g)
chop, raw	95	95	0	0	1 oz (30 g)

	Calories per 1 oz (30 g)	Calories per portion	Carbohydrate units per 1 oz (30 g)	Carbohydrate units per portion	Size of average portion
chop, grilled	95	565	0	0	1 chop
leg, raw	75	75	0	0	1 oz (30 g)
leg, roast	80	325	0	0	4 oz (114 g)
pork pie	105	420	$1\frac{1}{2}$	6	4 oz (114 g)
pork sausages					
fried	90	180	$\frac{3}{4}$	1	1 sausage
grilled	90	125	$\frac{3}{4}$	1	1 sausage
porridge	15	65	$\frac{1}{2}$	2	5 oz (142 g)
port	45	90	2	4	2 oz (57 ml)
port salut cheese	90	90	0	0	1 oz (30 g)
potato crisps all flavours	150	125	3	$2\frac{1}{2}$	1 small pkt
potato rings	150	150	$3\frac{1}{2}$	$3\frac{1}{2}$	1 oz (30 g)
potatoes					
old, boiled	25	100	1	4	4 oz (114 g)
old, mashed	35	140	1	4	4 oz (114 g)
old, baked	30	120	$1\frac{1}{2}$	6	1 small
old, roast	45	180	$1\frac{1}{2}$	6	2 small
chips, fresh	70	430	2	12	6 oz (171 g)
chips, frozen	30	30	1	1	1 oz (30 g)
chips, fried	80	495	2	10	6 oz (171 g)
new, boiled	20	85	1	4	4 oz (114 g)
new, canned	15	60	$\frac{3}{4}$	3	4 oz (114 g)
instant powder	90	90	4	4	1 oz (30 g)
instant, made up	20	80	1	4	4 oz (114 g)

	Calories per 1 oz (30 g)	Calories per portion	Carbohydrate units per 1 oz (30 g)	Carbohydrate units per portion	Size of average portion

POULTRY AND GAME

chicken

raw, meat only	35	35	o	o	1 oz (30 g)
raw, meat & skin	65	65	o	o	1 oz (30 g)
boiled					
meat only	50	255	o	o	5 oz (142 g)
light meat	45	230	o	o	5 oz (142 g)
dark meat	60	295	o	o	5 oz (142 g)
roast					
meat only	40	210	o	o	5 oz (142 g)
meat & skin	60	290	o	o	5 oz (142 g)
light meat	40	200	o	o	5 oz (142 g)
dark meat	45	220	o	o	5 oz (142 g)
wing quarter	20	65	o	o	1 medium
leg quarter	25	155	o	o	1 small

duck

raw, meat only	35	35	o	o	1 oz (30 g)
roast, meat only	55	270	o	o	5 oz (142 g)

goose

raw	65	65	o	o	1 oz (29 g)
roast	90	360	o	o	4 oz (114 g)

grouse, roast

	50	300	o	o	1 small

hare

raw	40	40	o	o	1 oz (30 g)
roast	55	215	o	o	4 oz (114 g)

	Calories per 1 oz (30 g)	Calories per portion	Carbohydrate units per 1 oz (30 g)	Carbohydrate units per portion	Size of average portion
stewed	55	320	0	0	6 oz (171 g)
partridge, roast	60	240	0	0	4 oz (114 g)
pheasant, roast	60	240	0	0	4 oz (114 g)
pigeon, roast	65	260	0	0	4 oz (114 g)
poussin					
roast or grilled	20	250	0	0	1 bird
fried	30	360	0	0	1 bird
quail					
grilled or roast	20	165	0	0	1 bird
fried	30	430	0	0	1 bird
rabbit					
raw	35	35	0	0	1 oz (30 g)
roast or grilled	45	170	0	0	4 oz (114 g)
fried or boiled	50	200	0	0	4 oz (114 g)
stewed	50	300	0	0	6 oz (171 g)
turkey					
raw, meat only	30	30	0	0	1 oz (30 g)
raw, meat & skin	40	40	0	0	1 oz (30 g)
roast					
meat only	40	160	0	0	4 oz (114 g)
meat & skin	50	200	0	0	4 oz (114 g)
light meat	35	150	0	0	4 oz (114 g)
dark meat	40	170	0	0	4 oz (114 g)
venison					
raw	40	40	0	0	1 oz (30 g)

	Calories per 1 oz (30 g)	Calories per portion	Carbohydrate units per 1 oz (30 g)	Carbohydrate units per portion	Size of average portion
roast	55	220	0	0	4 oz (114 g)
fried	65	250	0	0	4 oz (114 g)
grilled	55	225	0	0	4 oz (114 g)
woodcock, roast	20	160	0	0	1 bird
poussin					
roast or grilled	20	250	0	0	1 bird
fried	30	360	0	0	1 bird
prawns					
raw, in shells	10	10	0	0	1 oz (30 g)
raw, shelled	30	60	0	0	2 oz (57 g)
boiled	30	60	0	0	2 oz (57 g)
potted	120	240	0	0	2 oz (57 g)
processed cheese	90	90	0	0	1 oz (30 g)
prosciutto ham	65	65	0	0	1 oz (30 g)
prunes					
dried, raw	40	40	2	2	1 oz (30 g)
stewed, no sugar	25	95	1	4	4 oz (114 g)
stewed + sugar	30	120	$1\frac{1}{2}$	6	4 oz (114 g)
canned	25	100	$1\frac{1}{2}$	6	4 oz (114 g)
juice	20	110	1	5	$\frac{1}{4}$ pt (142 ml)
puffed wheat	95	95	4	4	1 oz (30 g)
pumpernickel	95	95	$3\frac{1}{2}$	$3\frac{1}{2}$	1 oz (30 g)
pumpkins					
raw	4	4	0	0	1 oz (30 g)
boiled	2	10	0	0	5 oz (142 g)

	Calories per 1 oz (30 g)	Calories per portion	Carbohydrate units per 1 oz (30 g)	Carbohydrate units per portion	Size of average portion
quail					
grilled or roast	20	165	0	0	1 bird
fried	30	430	0	0	1 bird
queen of puddings	60	360	2	8	6 oz (171 g)
quiche lorraine	110	440	1	4	small slice
quinces, raw	5	5	$\frac{1}{4}$	$\frac{1}{4}$	1 oz (30 g)

rabbit					
raw	35	35	0	0	1 oz (30 g)

	Calories per 1 oz (30 g)	Calories per portion	Carbohydrate units per 1 oz (30 g)	Carbohydrate units per portion	Size of average portion
grilled or roast	45	170	0	0	4 oz (114 g)
fried or boiled	50	200	0	0	4 oz (114 g)
stewed	50	300	0	0	6 oz (171 g)
radishes, raw	4	4	0	0	1 oz (30 g)
raisins, dried	70	70	$3\frac{1}{2}$	$3\frac{1}{2}$	1 oz (30 g)
raisin bran	100	100	$4\frac{1}{2}$	$4\frac{1}{2}$	1 oz (30 g)
raspberries					
raw	5	25	$\frac{1}{4}$	1	4 oz (114 g)
stewed, no sugar	5	25	$\frac{1}{4}$	1	4 oz (114 g)
stewed + sugar	20	80	1	4	4 oz (114 g)
canned	25	100	1	5	4 oz (114 g)
ratatouille	20	170	0	0	10 oz (284 g)
ravioli	70	400	$1\frac{1}{2}$	8	6 oz (171 g)
redcurrants					
raw	5	25	$\frac{1}{4}$	1	4 oz (114 g)
stewed, no sugar	5	20	$\frac{1}{4}$	1	4 oz (114 g)
stewed + sugar	15	60	$\frac{3}{4}$	3	4 oz (114 g)
jam	75	20	4	1	1 tsp
red kidney beans, cooked	25	100	1	4	4 oz (114 g)
retsina	20	100	1	5	$\frac{1}{4}$ pt (142 ml)
rhubarb					
raw	2	10	0	0	5 oz (142 g)
stewed, no sugar	2	10	0	0	5 oz (142 g)
stewed + sugar	15	60	$\frac{3}{4}$	3	5 oz (142 g)

	Calories per 1 oz (30 g)	Calories per portion	Carbohydrate units per 1 oz (30 g)	Carbohydrate units per portion	Size of average portion
canned	15	75	$\frac{1}{2}$	3	5 oz (142 g)
rhubarb pie	50	300	$1\frac{1}{2}$	$7\frac{1}{2}$	6 oz (171 g)
rice					
white, raw	105	105	5	5	1 oz (30 g)
white, boiled	35	35	$1\frac{1}{2}$	$1\frac{1}{2}$	1 oz (30 g)
brown, raw	100	100	5	5	1 oz (30 g)
brown, boiled	35	35	$1\frac{1}{2}$	$1\frac{1}{2}$	1 oz (30 g)
rice pudding	35	220	1	6	6 oz (171 g)
canned	25	150	$\frac{3}{4}$	5	6 oz (171 g)
ricotta cheese	70	70	0	0	1 oz (30 g)
rock bun	105	420	$3\frac{1}{2}$	14	1 bun
rock salmon, fried in batter	75	375	$\frac{1}{2}$	2	5 oz (142 g)
roe, cod					
fried	55	110	$\frac{3}{4}$	$1\frac{1}{2}$	2 oz (57 g)
smoked	30	30	0	0	1 oz (30 g)
roe, herring, fried	70	140	$\frac{1}{4}$	$\frac{1}{2}$	2 oz (57 g)
rollmops	70	280	0	0	4 oz (114 g)
rolls					
brown, crusty	80	160	$2\frac{1}{2}$	5	1 small
brown, soft	80	160	$2\frac{1}{2}$	5	1 small
white, crusty	80	160	$3\frac{1}{2}$	7	1 small
white, soft	85	170	3	6	1 small
starch reduced	110	25	$2\frac{1}{2}$	$\frac{1}{2}$	1 roll
roquefort cheese	100	100	0	0	1 oz (30 g)

	Calories per 1 oz (30 g)	Calories per portion	Carbohydrate units per 1 oz (30 g)	Carbohydrate units per portion	Size of average portion
rosehip syrup, undiluted	65	10	$3\frac{1}{2}$	1	1 tsp
rum, white or dark	65	65	3	3	1 oz (30 ml)
runner beans, boiled	5	20	0	0	4 oz (114 g)
rye crispbread	90	25	4	1	1 biscuit
rye bread					
light	70	70	3	3	1 oz (30 g)
dark	90	90	$3\frac{1}{2}$	$3\frac{1}{2}$	1 oz (30 g)
rye flour	95	95	$4\frac{1}{2}$	$4\frac{1}{2}$	1 oz (30 g)

safflower oil	255	255	0	0	1 oz (30 ml)
Saint Paulin cheese	90	90	0	0	1 oz (30 g)
sage derby cheese	110	110	0	0	1 oz (30 g)

	Calories per 1 oz (30 g)	Calories per portion	Carbohydrate units per 1 oz (30 g)	Carbohydrate units per portion	Size of average portion
sago pudding	35	220	1	6	6 oz (171 g)
salad cream	90	45	1	$\frac{1}{2}$	1 dsp
salami	140	280	0	0	2 oz (57 g)
salmon					
raw	50	50	0	0	1 oz (30 g)
steamed	55	280	0	0	5 oz (142 g)
fried	65	330	0	0	5 oz (142 g)
smoked	40	80	0	0	2 oz (57 g)
canned	45	90	0	0	2 oz (57 g)
salmon trout					
raw	50	50	0	0	1 oz (30 g)
poached	55	280	0	0	5 oz (142 g)
salsify					
raw	5	5	0	0	1 oz (30 g)
boiled	5	20	0	0	4 oz (114 g)
sandwich biscuit	145	95	4	$2\frac{1}{2}$	1 biscuit
sangria	20	100	1	5	$\frac{1}{4}$ pt (142 ml)
sardines canned in oil, drained	60	120	0	0	2 oz (57 g)
canned in tomato sauce	50	100	0	0	2 oz (57 g)
satsumas	5	20	0	1	1 medium
sauces					
béchamel	40	160	$\frac{1}{2}$	2	4 oz (114 g)

	Calories per 1 oz (30 g)	Calories per portion	Carbohydrate units per 1 oz (30 g)	Carbohydrate units per portion	Size of average portion
bolognese	40	240	$\frac{1}{4}$	1	6 oz (171 g)
bread	30	60	$\frac{3}{4}$	$1\frac{1}{2}$	2 oz (57 g)
brown, bottled	30	30	$1\frac{1}{2}$	$1\frac{1}{2}$	1 oz (30 g)
cheese	55	220	$\frac{1}{2}$	2	4 oz (114 g)
ketchup	30	30	1	1	1 oz (30 g)
onion	30	60	$\frac{1}{2}$	1	2 oz (57 g)
tomato	25	100	$\frac{1}{2}$	2	4 oz (114 g)
white, savoury	40	160	$\frac{1}{2}$	2	4 oz (114 g)
white, sweet	50	200	1	4	4 oz (114 g)
sauerkraut, canned	5	20	$\frac{1}{4}$	1	4 oz (114 g)
sausages					
beef, fried	75	150	$\frac{1}{2}$	1	1 sausage
beef, grilled	55	110	$\frac{1}{2}$	1	1 sausage
pork, fried	90	180	$\frac{3}{4}$	1	1 sausage
pork, grilled	90	125	$\frac{3}{4}$	1	1 sausage
liver	90	90	$\frac{1}{4}$	$\frac{1}{4}$	1 oz (30 g)
sausage roll					
flaky pastry	135	270	2	4	1 small
short pastry	110	220	2	4	1 small
saveloy	75	150	$\frac{1}{2}$	1	2 oz (57 g)
savouries					
cheese footballs	150	15	5	$\frac{1}{2}$	1 football
cheese straws	160	160	$1\frac{1}{2}$	$1\frac{1}{2}$	1 oz (30 g)
twiglets	100	5	8	$\frac{1}{2}$	1 twiglet
potato rings	150	150	$3\frac{1}{2}$	$3\frac{1}{2}$	1 oz (30 g)

	Calories per 1 oz (30 g)	Calories per portion	Carbohydrate units per 1 oz (30 g)	Carbohydrate units per portion	Size of average portion
scallops					
raw	30	30	0	0	1 oz (30 g)
steamed	30	90	0	0	2 fish
fried	35	115	0	0	2 fish
canned	30	90	0	0	3 oz (85 g)
scampi					
boiled	30	120	0	0	3 pieces
fried in batter	55	275	$\frac{1}{2}$	2	3 pieces
fried in breadcrumbs	90	450	2	8	3 pieces
schnapps	65	65	3	3	1 oz (30 ml)
screw driver	45	220	2	10	$\frac{1}{4}$ pt (142 ml)
scones					
plain	85	130	$2\frac{1}{2}$	4	1 medium
cheese	100	200	$2\frac{1}{2}$	$4\frac{1}{2}$	1 medium
currant	105	160	$3\frac{1}{2}$	5	1 medium
scotch egg	275	550	$\frac{3}{4}$	4	1 egg
scotch pancakes	80	120	2	3	1 medium
seakale, boiled	2	10	0	0	5 oz (142 g)
semi-skimmed milk	15	15	$\frac{1}{4}$	$\frac{1}{4}$	1 oz (30 ml)
semi sweet biscuit	130	50	$4\frac{1}{2}$	$1\frac{1}{2}$	1 biscuit
semolina					
raw	100	100	4	4	1 oz (30 g)
pudding	35	220	1	6	6 oz (171 g)
shandy	10	80	$\frac{3}{4}$	4	$\frac{1}{2}$ pt (284 ml)

	Calories per 1 oz (30 g)	Calories per portion	Carbohydrate units per 1 oz (30 g)	Carbohydrate units per portion	Size of average portion
shepherd's pie	35	350	$\frac{1}{2}$	5	10 oz (284 g)
sherry					
dry	35	70	$1\frac{1}{2}$	3	2 oz (57 ml)
medium	35	70	$1\frac{3}{4}$	$3\frac{1}{2}$	2 oz (57 ml)
sweet	40	80	2	4	2 oz (57 ml)
shortbread	145	95	$3\frac{1}{2}$	$2\frac{1}{2}$	1 biscuit
shortcrust pastry					
raw	130	130	$2\frac{1}{2}$	$2\frac{1}{2}$	1 oz (30 g)
cooked	150	150	3	3	1 oz (30 g)
shredded wheat	90	90	4	4	1 oz (30 g)
shrimps					
raw in shells	10	10	0	0	1 oz (30 g)
raw, shelled	30	60	0	0	2 oz (57 g)
boiled	30	60	0	0	2 oz (57 g)
potted	120	240	0	0	2 oz (57 g)
simnel cake	110	440	3	12	4 oz (114 g)
skate					
raw	20	20	0	0	1 oz (30 g)
steamed	25	130	0	0	5 oz (142 g)
fried in batter	35	170	$\frac{1}{2}$	3	6 oz (171 g)
fried in breadcrumbs	50	300	$\frac{1}{4}$	1	6 oz (171 g)
skimmed milk					
fresh	10	10	$\frac{1}{4}$	$\frac{1}{4}$	1 oz (30 ml)
dried	100	15	3	$\frac{1}{2}$	2 tsp
snails with butter	180	270	0	0	6 snails

	Calories per 1 oz (30 g)	Calories per portion	Carbohydrate units per 1 oz (30 g)	Carbohydrate units per portion	Size of average portion
soda bread	60	60	1	1	1 oz (30 g)
soda water	0	0	0	0	4 oz (114 ml)
sole, lemon or Dover					
raw	25	25	0	0	1 oz (30 g)
steamed	25	130	0	0	5 oz (142 g)
fried in breadcrumbs	60	310	0	$\frac{1}{2}$	5 oz (142 g)
soufflé, cheese	70	355	$\frac{1}{2}$	3	5 oz (142 g)

SOUP

chicken cream	15	140	0	2	$\frac{1}{2}$ pt (284 ml)
chicken noodle	5	55	0	2	$\frac{1}{2}$ pt (284 ml)
consommé	10	70	0	0	$\frac{1}{2}$ pt (284 ml)
French onion	30	270	$\frac{1}{2}$	4	$\frac{1}{2}$ pt (284 ml)
lentil	30	300	$\frac{3}{4}$	6	$\frac{1}{2}$ pt (284 ml)
minestrone	5	65	$\frac{1}{4}$	2	$\frac{1}{2}$ pt (284 ml)
mulligatawny	10	100	$\frac{1}{2}$	3	$\frac{1}{2}$ pt (284 ml)
mushroom	15	150	$\frac{1}{4}$	2	$\frac{1}{2}$ pt (284 ml)
oxtail	15	150	0	2	$\frac{1}{2}$ pt (284 ml)
tomato	15	150	$\frac{1}{4}$	3	$\frac{1}{2}$ pt (284 ml)
vegetable	10	100	$\frac{1}{4}$	4	$\frac{1}{2}$ pt (284 ml)
soured cream	55	55	0	0	1 oz (30 ml)
soya bean					
raw	115	115	2	2	1 oz (30 g)
cooked	10	40	$\frac{1}{4}$	1	4 oz (114 g)

	Calories per 1 oz (30 g)	Calories per portion	Carbohydrate units per 1 oz (30 g)	Carbohydrate units per portion	Size of average portion
soya flour					
full fat	130	130	$1\frac{1}{2}$	$1\frac{1}{2}$	1 oz (30 g)
low fat	100	100	2	2	1 oz (30 g)
soya oil	255	255	0	0	1 oz (30 ml)
spaghetti					
raw	105	105	5	5	1 oz (30 g)
boiled	35	200	$1\frac{1}{2}$	9	6 oz (171 g)
canned in tomato sauce	15	100	$\frac{3}{4}$	4	6 oz (171 g)
spinach					
raw	10	10	0	0	1 oz (30 g)
boiled	10	50	0	0	6 oz (171 g)
sponge biscuit, chocolate covered	150	50	6	2	1 biscuit
sponge cake					
with fat	130	260	3	6	2 oz (57 g)
fatless	85	170	3	6	2 oz (57 g)
with jam	85	170	$3\frac{1}{2}$	7	2 oz (57 g)
sponge pudding	100	400	$2\frac{1}{2}$	10	4 oz (114 g)
sprats					
raw	25	25	0	0	1 oz (30 g)
fried	125	500	0	0	4 oz (114 g)
fried in batter	125	500	$\frac{1}{2}$	2	4 oz (114 g)
spring greens					
raw	10	10	0	0	1 oz (30 g)

	Calories per 1 oz (30 g)	Calories per portion	Carbohydrate units per 1 oz (30 g)	Carbohydrate units per portion	Size of average portion
boiled	10	40	0	0	4 oz (114 g)
sprouts, Brussels					
raw	10	10	0	0	1 oz (30 g)
boiled	5	30	0	0	6 oz (171 g)
squash, lemon or orange, undiluted	30	30	$1\frac{1}{2}$	$1\frac{1}{2}$	1 oz (30 ml)
squid					
raw	20	20	0	0	1 oz (30 g)
steamed	25	125	0	0	5 oz (142 g)
fried	35	170	0	0	5 oz (142 g)
starch reduced crispbread	110	30	2	$\frac{1}{2}$	1 biscuit
starch reduced roll	110	25	$2\frac{1}{2}$	$\frac{1}{2}$	1 roll
steak & kidney pie					
single crust	80	640	1	8	8 oz (227 g)
individual	90	735	$1\frac{1}{2}$	11	8 oz (227 g)
sterilized milk	20	20	$\frac{1}{4}$	$\frac{1}{4}$	1 oz (30 ml)
stew, beef	35	340	$\frac{1}{4}$	2	10 oz (284 g)
stew, Irish	35	530	$\frac{1}{2}$	9	15 oz (426 g)
stewed steak with gravy	50	400	0	0	8 oz (227 g)
stilton cheese	130	130	0	0	1 oz (30 g)
stout, bottled	10	100	$\frac{1}{2}$	$5\frac{1}{2}$	$\frac{1}{2}$ pt (284 ml)
strawberries					
raw	10	45	$\frac{1}{4}$	2	6 oz (171 g)

	Calories per 1 oz (30 g)	Calories per portion	Carbohydrate units per 1 oz (30 g)	Carbohydrate units per portion	Size of average portion
canned	25	125	1	5	5 oz (142 g)
strawberry mousse, frozen	40	110	1	$2\frac{1}{2}$	$3\frac{1}{2}$ oz (100 g)
strong ale	20	200	1	10	$\frac{1}{2}$ pt (284 ml)
suet					
block	255	255	0	0	1 oz (30 g)
shredded	235	235	$\frac{3}{4}$	$\frac{3}{4}$	1 oz (30 g)
suet pudding, steamed	95	475	2	11	5 oz (142 g)
sugar, white or brown	110	20	6	1	1 tsp
sugar-coated puffed wheat	100	100	5	5	1 oz (30 g)
sultanas, dried	70	70	$3\frac{1}{2}$	$3\frac{1}{2}$	1 oz (30 g)
sultana cake	100	300	3	9	3 oz (85 g)
sunflower oil	255	255	0	0	1 oz (30 ml)
swedes					
raw	5	5	0	0	1 oz (30 g)
boiled	5	30	$\frac{1}{4}$	1	6 oz (171 g)
sweetbread					
lamb, raw	35	35	0	0	1 oz (30 g)
lamb, fried	65	260	$\frac{1}{4}$	1	4 oz (114 g)
sweetcorn					
on cob boiled	35	175	1	6	1 medium
canned	20	80	1	4	4 oz (114 g)

	Calories per 1 oz (30 g)	Calories per portion	Carbohydrate units per 1 oz (30 g)	Carbohydrate units per portion	Size of average portion
sweet potatoes					
raw	25	25	1	1	1 oz (30 g)
boiled	25	100	1	4	4 oz (114 g)
sweets, boiled	95	95	5	5	1 oz (30 g)

SWEETS & CHOCOLATES

after dinner mints	120	120	4	4	1 oz (30 g)
boiled sweets e.g. fruit drops, clear mints	95	95	5	5	1 oz (30 g)
chocolate egg, cream filled	45	170	$3\frac{1}{2}$	6	1 egg
fruit gums	50	50	$2\frac{1}{2}$	$2\frac{1}{2}$	1 oz (30 g)
fruit pastilles	70	70	$3\frac{1}{2}$	$3\frac{1}{2}$	1 oz (30 g)
fudge	130	130	$4\frac{1}{2}$	$4\frac{1}{2}$	1 oz (30 g)
jelly babies	100	100	5	5	1 oz (30 g)
liquorice					
gums	70	70	$3\frac{1}{2}$	$3\frac{1}{2}$	1 oz (30 g)
all sorts	90	90	4	4	1 oz (30 g)
sticks	85	85	4	4	1 oz (30 g)
marzipan	125	125	3	3	1 oz (30 g)
marshmallows	95	95	$4\frac{1}{2}$	$4\frac{1}{2}$	1 oz (30 g)
milk chocolate	150	150	$3\frac{1}{2}$	$3\frac{1}{2}$	1 oz (30 g)
+ brazil nuts	155	155	$2\frac{1}{2}$	$2\frac{1}{2}$	1 oz (30 g)

	Calories per 1 oz (30 g)	Calories per portion	Carbohydrate units per 1 oz (30 g)	Carbohydrate units per portion	Size of average portion
+ fruit & nuts	140	140	3	3	1 oz (30 g)
+ wholenut	165	165	3	3	1 oz (30 g)
milk chocolate covered caramel bar	135	270	3	$5\frac{1}{2}$	2 oz (57 g) bar
caramel & fudge	135	270	4	$7\frac{1}{2}$	2 oz (57 g) bar
caramel & nuts	150	225	$3\frac{1}{2}$	$5\frac{1}{2}$	$1\frac{1}{2}$ oz (43 g) bar
coconut bar	140	140	3	3	1 oz (30 g)
fudge	125	125	$3\frac{1}{2}$	$3\frac{1}{2}$	1 finger
wafer biscuit	145	110	$3\frac{1}{2}$	$2\frac{1}{2}$	2 wafers
peppermints	110	110	6	6	1 oz (30 g)
peppermint creams	100	100	$5\frac{1}{2}$	$5\frac{1}{2}$	1 oz (30 g)
plain chocolate covered	120	120	4	4	1 oz (30 g)
plain chocolate	150	150	$3\frac{1}{2}$	$3\frac{1}{2}$	1 oz (30 g)
+ almonds	160	160	3	3	1 oz (30 g)
covered peppermint cream bar	130	130	4	4	1 oz (30 g) bar
toffees assorted	120	120	4	4	1 oz (30 g)
chocolate coated, assorted	130	130	$3\frac{1}{2}$	$3\frac{1}{2}$	1 oz (30 g)
Swiss roll	75	290	3	12	4 oz (114 g)
syrup, golden	85	85	$4\frac{1}{2}$	$4\frac{1}{2}$	1 tbsp

	Calories per 1 oz (30 g)	Calories per portion	Carbohydrate units per 1 oz (30 g)	Carbohydrate units per portion	Size of average portion
tagliatelle					
raw	105	105	5	5	1 oz (30 g)
boiled	35	200	$1\frac{1}{2}$	9	6 oz (171 g)
tangerine	5	20	$\frac{1}{4}$	1	1 medium
canned	15	60	1	3	4 oz (114 g)
tapioca					
raw	100	100	5	5	1 oz (30 g)
pudding	35	220	1	4	4 oz (114 g)
taramasalata	90	180	$\frac{1}{2}$	1	2 oz (57 g)
tart, custard	95	370	2	7	4 oz (114 g)
tart, jam	120	120	$3\frac{1}{2}$	$3\frac{1}{2}$	1 tart
tartare sauce	140	140	0	0	1 oz (30 g)
teacake	85	170	3	6	1 teacake
Tia Maria	90	90	3	3	1 oz (30 ml)

	Calories per 1 oz (30 g)	Calories per portion	Carbohydrate units per 1 oz (30 g)	Carbohydrate units per portion	Size of average portion
toast, white	85	85	$3\frac{1}{2}$	$3\frac{1}{2}$	1 oz (30 g)
toffees, mixed	120	120	4	4	1 oz (30 g)
Tom Collins	25	250	$\frac{3}{4}$	8	$\frac{1}{2}$ pt (284 ml)
tomatoes					
raw	4	15	O	O	1 medium
fried	20	80	O	O	1 medium
chutney	45	45	2	2	1 oz (30 g)
juice	4	20	O	1	$\frac{1}{4}$ pt (142 ml)
ketchup	30	30	1	1	1 oz (30 g)
purée	20	20	$\frac{3}{4}$	$\frac{3}{4}$	1 oz (30 g)
sauce	25	100	$\frac{1}{2}$	2	4 oz (114 g)
soup, canned	15	150	$\frac{1}{4}$	3	$\frac{1}{2}$ pt (284 ml)
tomé au raisin	80	80	O	O	1 oz (30 g)
tongue					
lamb, raw	55	55	O	O	1 oz (30 g)
sheep, stewed	80	490	O	O	6 oz (171 g)
ox, pickled	60	60	O	O	1 oz (30 g)
ox, boiled	85	170	O	O	2 oz (57 g)
canned	60	120	O	O	2 oz (57 g)
tonic water	5	20	$\frac{1}{4}$	1	4 oz (114 ml)
treacle, black	75	35	4	2	1 tbsp
treacle tart	105	420	$3\frac{1}{2}$	14	4 oz (114 g)
trifle	45	370	1	7	6 oz (171 g)
tripe					
dressed	15	15	O	O	1 oz (30 g)

	Calories per 1 oz (30 g)	Calories per portion	Carbohydrate units per 1 oz (30 g)	Carbohydrate units per portion	Size of average portion
stewed	30	180	o	o	6 oz (171 g)
trout					
raw	25	25	o	o	1 oz (30 g)
steamed	25	200	o	o	1 small
fried	40	320	o	o	1 small
smoked	25	200	o	o	1 small
tuna canned in oil, drained	80	160	o	o	1 small can
turbot					
raw	20	20	o	o	1 oz (30 g)
steamed	30	140	o	o	5 oz (142 g)
fried in breadcrumbs	50	250	$\frac{1}{4}$	1	5 oz (142 g)
turkey					
raw, meat only	30	30	o	o	1 oz (30 g)
raw, meat & skin	40	40	o	o	1 oz (30 g)
roast meat only	40	160	o	o	4 oz (114 g)
meat & skin	50	200	o	o	4 oz (114 g)
light meat	35	150	o	o	4 oz (114 g)
dark meat	40	170	o	o	4 oz (114 g)
turnips					
raw	5	5	o	o	1 oz (30 g)
boiled	4	25	o	$\frac{3}{4}$	6 oz (171 g)
turnip tops, boiled	3	20	o	o	6 oz (171 g)

	Calories per 1 oz (30 g)	Calories per portion	Carbohydrate units per 1 oz (30 g)	Carbohydrate units per portion	Size of average portion
veal cutlet					
fried	60	365	$\frac{1}{4}$	$1\frac{1}{2}$	1 cutlet
fillet raw	30	30	0	0	1 oz (30 g)
roast	65	260	0	0	4 oz (114 g)
jellied	35	140	0	0	4 oz (114 g)
VEGETABLES					
ackee, canned	45	180	0	0	4 oz (114 g)
artichokes					
globe, boiled	5	10	$\frac{1}{4}$	$\frac{1}{2}$	1 medium
heart, boiled	4	15	0	$\frac{1}{2}$	4 oz (114 g)
heart, canned	4	15	0	$\frac{1}{2}$	4 oz (114 g)
Jerusalem, boiled	5	20	$\frac{1}{4}$	1	4 oz (114 g)
asparagus					
boiled	5	20	0	$\frac{1}{4}$	4 oz (114 g)

	Calories per 1 oz (30 g)	Calories per portion	Carbohydrate units per 1 oz (30 g)	Carbohydrate units per portion	Size of average portion
canned	3	10	0	$\frac{1}{4}$	4 oz (114 g)
aubergine					
fried	35	140	$\frac{1}{4}$	1	4 oz (114 g)
baked	25	100	$\frac{1}{4}$	1	4 oz (114 g)
avocado pear	65	250	0	$\frac{1}{2}$	$\frac{1}{2}$ large
bamboo shoots, canned	10	10	$\frac{1}{4}$	$\frac{1}{4}$	1 oz (30 g)
beans					
French, boiled	2	10	0	0	5 oz (142 g)
runner, boiled	5	20	0	0	4 oz (114 g)
baked	20	100	$\frac{1}{2}$	3	5 oz (142 g)
broad, boiled	15	60	$\frac{1}{2}$	2	4 oz (114 g)
butter, boiled	25	100	1	4	4 oz (114 g)
haricot, boiled	25	100	1	4	4 oz (114 g)
mung, raw	65	65	2	2	1 oz (30 g)
mung, cooked	30	60	$\frac{3}{4}$	$1\frac{1}{2}$	2 oz (57 g)
red kidney, cooked	25	100	1	4	4 oz (114 g)
soya, raw	115	115	2	2	1 oz (30 g)
soya, cooked	10	40	$\frac{1}{4}$	1	4 oz (114 g)
beansprouts					
raw or boiled	3	15	0	0	5 oz (142 g)
canned	5	25	0	0	5 oz (142 g)
beetroot, boiled	15	30	$\frac{1}{2}$	1	2 oz (57 g)
broccoli tops, boiled	5	20	0	0	4 oz (114 g)

	Calories per 1 oz (30 g)	Calories per portion	Carbohydrate units per 1 oz (30 g)	Carbohydrate units per portion	Size of average portion
Brussels sprouts, boiled	5	30	O	O	6 oz (171 g)
cabbage					
red, raw	5	20	O	O	3 oz (85 g)
red, boiled	4	15	O	O	4 oz (114 g)
red, pickled	5	5	O	O	1 oz (30 g)
savoy, boiled	3	10	O	O	4 oz (114 g)
white, raw	3	10	O	O	4 oz (114 g)
white, boiled	4	15	O	O	4 oz (114 g)
capers	O	O	O	O	1 oz (30 g)
carrots					
old, raw or boiled	5	20	$\frac{1}{4}$	1	4 oz (114 g)
young, raw	5	30	$\frac{1}{2}$	1	4 oz (114 g)
young, boiled	4	15	$\frac{1}{4}$	1	4 oz (114 g)
young, canned	5	20	$\frac{1}{4}$	1	4 oz (114 g)
juice	5	25	$\frac{1}{2}$	2	$\frac{1}{4}$ pt (142 ml)
cauliflower					
raw	4	15	O	O	4 oz (114 g)
boiled	3	10	O	O	4 oz (114 g)
pickled	3	3	O	O	1 oz (30 g)
celeriac					
raw	5	10	O	O	2 oz (57 g)
boiled	4	15	O	O	4 oz (114 g)
celery					
raw	2	5	O	O	2 oz (57 g)

	Calories per 1 oz (30 g)	Calories per portion	Carbohydrate units per 1 oz (30 g)	Carbohydrate units per portion	Size of average portion
boiled	2	5	0	0	2 oz (57 g)
canned	1	5	0	0	4 oz (114 g)
chicory					
raw	3	5	0	0	2 oz (57 g)
boiled	3	10	0	0	4 oz (114 g)
corn on cob, boiled	35	175	1	6	1 medium
courgette					
raw	3	3	0	0	1 oz (30 g)
boiled	1	5	0	$\frac{1}{4}$	4 oz (114 g)
fried	35	140	0	$\frac{1}{2}$	4 oz (114 g)
cucumber					
raw	3	3	0	0	1 oz (30 g)
pickled	3	3	$\frac{1}{4}$	$\frac{1}{4}$	1 oz (30 g)
endive					
raw	3	5	0	0	2 oz (57 g)
boiled	3	10	0	0	4 oz (114 g)
garlic	5	1	0	0	1 clove
horseradish, raw	15	15	$\frac{1}{2}$	$\frac{1}{2}$	1 oz (30 g)
laverbread	15	15	0	0	1 oz (30 g)
leeks					
raw	10	10	0	0	1 oz (30 g)
boiled	5	30	0	0	4 oz (114 g)
lentils					
raw	85	85	3	3	1 oz (30 g)
split boiled	30	120	1	4	4 oz (114 g)

	Calories per 1 oz (30 g)	Calories per portion	Carbohydrate units per 1 oz (30 g)	Carbohydrate units per portion	Size of average portion
lettuce, raw	3	10	0	0	3 oz (85 g)
marrow					
raw	3	3	0	0	1 oz (30 g)
boiled	1	5	0	0	4 oz (114 g)
mushrooms					
raw	4	4	0	0	1 oz (30 g)
boiled	2	5	0	0	2 oz (57 g)
fried	60	120	0	0	2 oz (57 g)
mustard & cress	3	3	0	0	1 oz (30 g)
okra					
raw	5	5	0	0	1 oz (30 g)
boiled or canned	5	20	0	0	4 oz (114 g)
olives					
black or green	25	25	0	0	10 olives
stuffed	30	30	0	0	10 olives
onions					
raw	5	5	0	0	1 oz (30 g)
boiled	4	15	0	0	4 oz (114 g)
fried	100	100	$\frac{1}{2}$	$\frac{1}{2}$	1 oz (30 g)
spring, raw	10	3	0	0	1 onion
palm heart, canned	30	120	$1\frac{1}{2}$	6	4 oz (114 g)
parsley, raw	5	5	0	0	1 oz (30 g)
parsnips, boiled	15	60	$\frac{3}{4}$	3	4 oz (114 g)
peas					
fresh, raw	20	20	$\frac{1}{2}$	$\frac{1}{2}$	1 oz (30 g)

	Calories per 1 oz (30 g)	Calories per portion	Carbohydrate units per 1 oz (30 g)	Carbohydrate units per portion	Size of average portion
boiled	15	45	$\frac{1}{2}$	1	3 oz (85 g)
frozen, raw	15	15	$\frac{1}{2}$	$\frac{1}{2}$	1 oz (30 g)
boiled	10	30	$\frac{1}{4}$	1	3 oz (85 g)
canned, garden	15	45	$\frac{1}{2}$	1	3 oz (85 g)
canned, processed	25	65	$\frac{3}{4}$	3	3 oz (85 g)
dried, raw	80	80	3	3	1 oz (30 g)
dried, boiled	30	90	1	3	3 oz (85 g)
split, raw	90	90	3	3	1 oz (30 g)
split, boiled	35	105	1	4	3 oz (85 g)
chick, raw	90	90	3	3	1 oz (30 g)
chick, boiled	40	160	1	4	4 oz (114 g)
red pigeon, raw	85	85	3	3	1 oz (30 g)
red pigeon, cooked	30	90	1	3	3 oz (85 g)
peppers					
raw	4	10	0	0	2 oz (57 g)
boiled	4	10	0	0	2 oz (57 g)
plantain green					
boiled	35	140	2	7	4 oz (114 g)
ripe, fried	75	300	$2\frac{1}{2}$	7	4 oz (114 g)
potatoes					
old, boiled	25	100	1	4	4 oz (114 g)
old, mashed	35	140	1	4	4 oz (114 g)
old, baked	30	120	$1\frac{1}{2}$	6	1 small
old, roast	45	180	$1\frac{1}{2}$	6	2 small
chips, fresh	70	430	2	12	6 oz (171 g)

	Calories per 1 oz (30 g)	Calories per portion	Carbohydrate units per 1 oz (30 g)	Carbohydrate units per portion	Size of average portion
chips, frozen	30	30	1	1	1 oz (30 g)
chips, fried	80	495	2	10	6 oz (171 g)
new, boiled	20	85	1	4	4 oz (114 g)
new, canned	15	60	$\frac{3}{4}$	3	4 oz (114 g)
instant, powder	90	90	4	4	1 oz (30 g)
instant, made up	20	80	1	4	4 oz (114 g)
crisps	150	125	3	$2\frac{1}{2}$	small pkt
pumpkin					
raw	4	4	0	0	1 oz (30 g)
boiled	2	10	0	0	5 oz (142 g)
radishes, raw	4	4	0	0	1 oz (30 g)
salsify					
raw	5	5	0	0	1 oz (30 g)
boiled	5	20	0	0	4 oz (114 g)
sauerkraut, canned	5	20	$\frac{1}{4}$	1	4 oz (114 g)
seakale, boiled	2	10	0	0	5 oz (142 g)
spinach					
raw	10	10	0	0	1 oz (30 g)
boiled	10	50	0	0	6 oz (171 g)
spring greens					
raw	10	10	0	0	1 oz (30 g)
boiled	10	40	0	0	4 oz (114 g)
swedes					
raw	5	5	0	0	1 oz (30 g)
boiled	5	30	$\frac{1}{4}$	1	6 oz (171 g)

	Calories per 1 oz (30 g)	Calories per portion	Carbohydrate units per 1 oz (30 g)	Carbohydrate units per portion	Size of average portion
sweet corn canned	20	80	I	4	4 oz (114 g)
sweet potatoes					
raw	25	25	I	I	I oz (30 g)
boiled	25	100	I	4	4 oz (114 g)
tomatoes					
raw	4	15	O	O	I medium
fried	20	80	O	O	I medium
juice	4	20	O	I	$\frac{1}{4}$ pt (142 ml)
turnips					
raw	5	5	O	O	I oz (30 g)
boiled	4	25	O	$\frac{3}{4}$	6 oz (171 g)
turnip tops, boiled	3	20	O	O	6 oz (171 g)
watercress, raw	4	4	O	O	I oz (30 g)
yam					
raw	35	35	2	2	I oz (30 g)
boiled	35	205	2	10	6 oz (171 g)
vegetable oils	255	255	O	O	I oz (30 ml)
vegetable soup	10	100	$\frac{1}{4}$	4	$\frac{1}{2}$ pt (284 ml)
venison					
raw	40	40	O	O	I oz (30 g)
roast	55	220	O	O	4 oz (114 g)
fried	65	250	O	O	4 oz (114 g)
grilled	55	225	O	O	4 oz (114 g)
vermouth					
dry	35	70	2	4	2 oz (57 ml)

	Calories per 1 oz (30 g)	Calories per portion	Carbohydrate units per 1 oz (30 g)	Carbohydrate units per portion	Size of average portion
sweet	45	90	$2\frac{1}{2}$	5	2 oz (57 ml)
vodka	65	65	3	3	1 oz (30 ml)
vodka cocktail	50	160	2	6	3 oz (85 ml)

wafers	75	10	15	3	1 wafer
wafer biscuit filled	150	70	4	$1\frac{1}{2}$	1 wafer
walnuts shelled	150	150	$\frac{1}{4}$	$\frac{1}{4}$	1 oz (30 g)
water biscuit	125	60	$4\frac{1}{2}$	2	1 biscuit
water cress	4	4	0	0	1 oz (30 g)
water melon	5	50	$\frac{1}{4}$	3	large slice
Welsh rarebit	105	420	1	$4\frac{1}{2}$	4 oz (114 g)
wensleydale cheese	110	110	0	0	1 oz (30 g)
wheatgerm	100	50	3	$1\frac{1}{2}$	$\frac{1}{2}$ oz (14 g)
whelks					
boiled in shells	4	4	0	0	1 oz (30 g)
shelled	25	75	0	0	3 oz (85 g)
whisky	65	65	3	3	1 oz (30 ml)

	Calories per 1 oz (30 g)	Calories per portion	Carbohydrate units per 1 oz (30 g)	Carbohydrate units per portion	Size of average portion
whisky sour	55	240	$2\frac{1}{2}$	11	$4\frac{1}{2}$ oz (128 ml)
whitebait					
raw	15	15	0	0	1 oz (30 g)
fried in batter	150	590	$\frac{1}{2}$	2	4 oz (114 g)
fried in flour	150	590	$\frac{1}{4}$	1	4 oz (114 g)
whitecurrants					
raw	5	30	$\frac{1}{4}$	1	4 oz (114 g)
stewed, no sugar	5	25	$\frac{1}{4}$	1	4 oz (114 g)
stewed + sugar	15	60	1	3	4 oz (114 g)
white pudding	130	255	2	4	2 oz (57 g)
white sauce					
savoury	40	160	$\frac{1}{2}$	2	4 oz (114 g)
sweet	50	200	1	4	4 oz (114 g)
whiting					
fried	55	275	$\frac{1}{2}$	2	5 oz (142 g)
steamed	25	130	0	0	5 oz (142 g)
wholemeal bread	60	60	$2\frac{1}{2}$	$2\frac{1}{2}$	1 oz (30 g)
wholemeal flour	90	90	$3\frac{1}{2}$	$3\frac{1}{2}$	1 oz (30 g)
wine					
red	20	100	1	5	$\frac{1}{4}$ pt (142 ml)
rosé	20	100	1	5	$\frac{1}{4}$ pt (142 ml)
white, dry	20	100	1	5	$\frac{1}{4}$ pt (142 ml)
white, medium	20	100	1	5	$\frac{1}{4}$ pt (142 ml)
white, sweet	25	125	$1\frac{1}{2}$	7	$\frac{1}{4}$ pt (142 ml)
white, sparkling	20	100	1	5	$\frac{1}{4}$ pt (142 ml)

	Calories per 1 oz (30 g)	Calories per portion	Carbohydrate units per 1 oz (30 g)	Carbohydrate units per portion	Size of average portion
winkles					
boiled in shell	4	4	0	0	1 oz (30 g)
shelled	20	60	0	0	3 oz (85 g)
woodcock, roast	20	160	0	0	1 bird

yam, boiled	35	205	2	10	6 oz (171 g)
yeast					
fresh	15	15	0	0	1 oz (30 g)
dried	50	50	0	0	1 oz (30 g)
yeast extract	50	5	0	0	$\frac{1}{2}$ tsp
yogurt, low fat					
natural	15	75	$\frac{1}{4}$	1	small carton
sweetened	25	130	1	$4\frac{1}{2}$	small carton
flavoured	25	125	$\frac{3}{4}$	4	small carton
fruit	30	135	1	5	small carton
hazelnut	30	150	1	5	small carton
yorkshire pudding	60	120	$1\frac{1}{2}$	3	1 small

TABLE 2

Foods in this section have been listed in numerical groups so that you can select an item with a particular carbohydrate content or within a certain Calorie range. The amounts given are for average portions. The Calorie groups come first on page 151, followed by the carbohydrate unit groups starting on page 167.

Meat, fish and green vegetables have been omitted from the 'carbohydrate unit' lists (unless they have been cooked in batter or breadcrumbs) as they contain no carbohydrate.

1—10

Apricots	1 medium
Artichokes, globe boiled	1 medium
Asparagus, canned	4 oz (114 g)
Bamboo shoots, canned	1 oz (30 g)
Beef extract, concentrated	1 tsp
Brown sauce, bottled	1 tsp
Cabbage, red pickled	1 oz (30 g)
Cabbage, savoy boiled	4 oz (114 g)
Cabbage, white raw	4 oz (114 g)
Capers	1 oz (30 g)
Cauliflower, boiled	4 oz (114 g)
Cauliflower, pickled	1 oz (30 g)
Celeriac, raw	2 oz (57 g)
Celery, raw, boiled or canned	4 oz (114 g)
Cherries, glacé	1 cherry
Chicory, raw	2 oz (57 g)
Chicory, boiled	4 oz (114 g)
Clementine	1 small
Coconut milk	2 oz (57 ml)
Coffee & chicory essence	1 tsp
Coffee, ground	1 cup
Coffee, instant	1 cup
Courgette, boiled	4 oz (114 g)
Cranberries, raw	1 oz (30 g)
Cucumber, raw or pickled	1 oz (30 g)
Endive, raw	2 oz (57 g)
Endive, boiled	4 oz (114 g)
Fish paste	1 tsp
French beans, boiled	5 oz (142 g)
Garlic	1 clove
Ice cream wafer	1 wafer
Ladies fingers, boiled or canned	4 oz (114 g)
Lemon juice, fresh	1 oz (30 ml)
Lettuce, raw	3 oz (85 g)
Marrow, boiled	4 oz (114 g)
Medlars, raw	1 large

Milk, cows' skimmed	1 oz (30 ml)
Mushrooms, raw or boiled	1 oz (30 g)
Onions, raw, or spring onions	1 oz (30 g)
Parsley, raw	1 oz (30 g)
Peppers, raw or boiled	2 oz (57 g)
Piccalilli	1 oz (30 g)
Pickled onions	1 oz (30 g)
Plums, fresh raw	1 medium
Pumpkins, boiled	5 oz (142 g)
Quinces, raw	1 oz (30 g)
Radishes, raw	1 oz (30 g)
Rhubarb, raw or stewed no sugar	5 oz (142 g)
Rosehip syrup, undiluted	1 tsp
Seakale, boiled	5 oz (142 g)
Skimmed milk, fresh	1 oz (30 ml)
Spinach, raw	1 oz (30 g)
Twiglets	1 twiglet
Wafers	1 wafer
Watercress	1 oz (30 g)
Whelks, boiled in shells	1 oz (30 g)
Yeast extract, concentrated	$\frac{1}{2}$ tsp

11—20

Apricot jam	1 tsp
Artichokes, hearts boiled or canned	4 oz (114 g)
Artichokes, Jerusalem boiled	4 oz (114 g)
Asparagus, boiled	4 oz (114 g)
Beansprouts, raw or boiled	5 oz (142 g)
Blackberry jam	1 tsp
Blackcurrant jam or jelly	1 tsp
Bran, wheat	1 tbsp

Broccoli tops, boiled	4 oz (114 g)
Cabbage, red raw	3 oz (85 g)
Cabbage, red boiled	4 oz (114 g)
Cabbage, white boiled	4 oz (114 g)
Carrots, old raw or boiled	4 oz (114 g)
Carrots, young boiled or canned	4 oz (114 g)
Cauliflower, raw	4 oz (114 g)
Celeriac, boiled	4 oz (114 g)
Cheese football savouries	1 football
Cherry jam	1 tsp
Cocoa powder	1 tsp
Cornflour	1 tsp
Cranberry sauce or jelly	1 dsp
Dried milk, skimmed	2 tsp
Figs, green raw	1 fig
Gelatine	1 tsp
Glucose	1 tsp
Gravy browning powder	1 tsp
Gooseberries, green, raw or stewed no sugar	4 oz (114 g)
Grapefruit, fresh	½ medium
Greengages, raw	1 fruit
Grissini	1 stick
Honey, in jars	1 tsp
Jam, all kinds	1 tsp
Kohlrabi, boiled	5 oz (142 g)
Laverbread	1 oz (30 g)
Lemons, whole	1 medium
Lemon curd	1 tsp
Loganberries, raw or stewed no sugar	4 oz (114 g)
Low fat spread	1 tsp
Lychees, raw	1 oz (30 g)
Marmalade	1 tsp
Milk, cows' whole, sterilized, longlife	1 oz (30 ml)
Milk, cows' dried skimmed	2 tsp
Milk, goats	1 oz (30 ml)
Milk, semi-skimmed (light)	1 oz (30 ml)
Mustard (powder)	1 tsp

Mustard cress	1 oz (30 g)
Okra, boiled or canned	4 oz (114 g)
Onions, boiled	4 oz (114 g)
Parmesan cheese	2 tsp
Runner beans	4 oz (114 g)
Salsify, boiled	4 oz (114 g)
Satsumas	1 medium
Sauerkraut, canned	4 oz (114 g)
Skimmed milk	2 tsp
Sugar, brown or white	1 tsp
Tangerine	1 medium
Tomatoes, raw	1 medium
Tomato juice	¼ pt (142 ml)
Tomato purée	1 oz (30 g)
Tonic water	4 oz (114 ml)
Turnip tops, boiled	6 oz (171 g)
Yeast, fresh	1 oz (30 g)

21–30

Apple sauce	2 oz (57 g)
Beansprouts, canned	5 oz (142 g)
Beetroot	2 oz (57 g)
Blackberries, stewed no sugar	4 oz (114 g)
Blackcurrants, stewed no sugar	4 oz (114 g)
Bombay duck, dried	1 fish
Brussels sprouts, boiled	6 oz (171 g)
Carrots, young raw	4 oz (114 g)
Carrot juice	¼ pt (142 ml)
Cockles, shelled boiled or canned	2 oz (57 g)
Cod's roe, smoked	1 oz (30 g)
Crispbread, rye or starch reduced	1 biscuit
Curd cheese	1 oz (30 g)

Ginger ale	4 oz (114 ml)
Horseradish sauce	1 dsp
Ice cream cone	1 cone
Leeks, boiled	4 oz (114 g)
Lemon squash, undiluted	1 oz (30 ml)
Lime juice, undiluted	1 oz (30 ml)
Mandarin, raw	1 small
Melons, honeydew	1 medium slice
Melons, ogen	½ medium
Mint sauce, in jars, undiluted	1 oz (30 g)
Olives, black, green or stuffed	10 olives
Orange squash, undiluted	1 oz (30 ml)
Peas, frozen boiled	3 oz (85 g)
Plums, stewed no sugar	4 oz (114 g)
Raspberries, raw or stewed no sugar	4 oz (114 g)
Redcurrants, raw or stewed no sugar	4 oz (114 g)
Swedes, boiled	6 oz (171 g)
Tomato ketchup	1 oz (30 g)
Turnips, boiled	6 oz (171 g)
Whitecurrants, raw or stewed no sugar	4 oz (114 g)

31—40

Apricot, stewed no sugar	5 oz (142 g)
Barley, pearl boiled	1 oz (30 g)
Bitter lemon	4 oz (114 ml)
Blackberries, raw	4 oz (114 g)
Blackcurrants, raw	4 oz (114 g)
Bombay duck, fried	1 fish
Cod liver oil	1 tsp
Cream crackers	1 cracker
Damsons, raw or stewed no sugar	4 oz (114 g)
Dried milk, whole	2 tsp
Drinking chocolate	2 tsp
Madeira	1 oz (30 ml)
Malted milk powder	2 tsp
Melons, cantaloupe	1 medium slice
Milk, cows' dried whole	2 tsp
Mulberries, raw	4 oz (114 g)
Oranges, segments	4 oz (114 g)
Oranges, whole	1 large
Passion fruit, raw	4 oz (114 g)
Peaches, fresh raw	1 large

Peaches, stewed no sugar	4 oz (114 g)
Pears, stewed no sugar	4 oz (114 g)
Pickle, sweet	1 oz (30 g)
Prunes, dried raw	1 oz (30 g)
Rice, white or brown boiled	1 oz (30 g)
Soya beans, cooked	4 oz (114 g)
Spring greens, boiled	4 oz (114 g)
Treacle, black	1 tbsp

41—50

Apples, stewed no sugar	5 oz (142 g)
Apricots, dried	1 oz (30 g)
Beer, draught mild	$\frac{1}{2}$ pt (284 ml)
Butter	1 pat
Buttermilk	$\frac{1}{4}$ pt (142 ml)
Cherries, raw or stewed, no sugar	4 oz (114 g)

Chocolate covered sponge biscuit	1 biscuit
Coconut biscuit	1 biscuit
Crisped rice breakfast cereal	$\frac{1}{2}$ oz (14 g)
Evaporated milk, whole unsweetened	1 oz (30 ml)
Figs, dried raw	1 fig
Flaked wheat biscuit	1 biscuit
Fruit gums	1 oz (30 g)
Gooseberries, ripe raw	4 oz (114 g)
Grapefruit juice, unsweetened	$\frac{1}{4}$ pt (142 ml)
Greengages, stewed, no sugar	4 oz (114 g)
Fruit shortcake biscuit	1 biscuit
Margarine	1 tsp
Meringue	1 large
Milk, cows' evaporated whole unsweetened	1 oz (30 ml)
Nectarines, raw	1 medium
Orange juice, fresh or canned, no sugar	$\frac{1}{4}$ pt (142 ml)
Oysters, canned	6 oysters

Oysters, smoked	3 oz (85 g)
Pears, raw	1 small
Peas, fresh boiled or garden canned	3 oz (85 g)
Salad cream	1 dsp
Semi sweet biscuit	1 biscuit
Spinach, boiled	6 oz (171 g)
Strawberries, raw	6 oz (171 g)
Tomato chutney	1 oz (30 g)
Watermelon	1 large slice
Wheatgerm	½ oz (14 g)
Yeast, dried	1 oz (30 g)

51–60

Anchovy, canned in oil or brine	1 oz (30 g)
Apples	1 medium
Apple chutney	1 oz (30 g)
Apples, baked with sugar	6 oz (171 g)
Bourbon biscuit	1 biscuit
Broad beans, boiled	4 oz (114 g)
Caviar, red, black or grey	1 oz (30 g)
Chicken noodle soup	½ pt (284 ml)
Clam, steamed or canned	2 oz (57 g)
Crayfish, shelled	2 oz (57 g)
Cream, soured	1 oz (30 ml)
Custard cream biscuit	1 biscuit
Gooseberries, green stewed with sugar	4 oz (114 g)
Grapefruit juice, sweetened	¼ pt (142 ml)
Guava, canned	4 oz (114 g)
High protein corn flakes	½ oz (14 g)
Lemonade, bottled	½ pt (284 ml)

Loganberries, stewed with sugar	4 oz (114 g)
Mandarin, canned	4 oz (114 g)
Mung beans, cooked (dahl)	2 oz (57 g)
Mussels, canned	3 oz (85 g)
Oatcakes	1 biscuit
Palmier	1 biscuit
Parsnips, boiled	4 oz (114 g)
Peaches, dried raw	1 oz (30 g)
Pineapple, fresh	4 oz (114 g)
Potatoes, new canned	4 oz (114 g)
Redcurrants, stewed with sugar	4 oz (114 g)
Rhubarb, stewed with sugar	5 oz (142 g)
Shrimps, boiled	2 oz (57 g)
Soda bread	1 oz (30 g)
Tangerines, canned	4 oz (114 g)
Tongue, ox pickled	1 oz (30 g)
Water biscuit	1 biscuit
Whitecurrants, stewed with sugar	4 oz (114 g)
Wholemeal bread	1 oz (30 g)
Winkles, shelled boiled	3 oz (85 g)

61–70

Anisette	1 oz (30 ml)
Apple juice, natural	¼ pt (142 ml)
Armagnac	1 oz (30 ml)
Bilberries, raw	4 oz (114 g)
Blackberries, stewed with sugar	4 oz (114 g)
Blackberries, canned in syrup	4 oz (114 g)
Blackcurrants, stewed with sugar	4 oz (114 g)
Blackcurrant juice, undiluted	1 oz (30 ml)

Blackcurrant liqueur	1 oz (30 ml)
Bourbon	1 oz (30 ml)
Butter biscuit	1 biscuit
Calvados	1 oz (30 ml)
Cassis	1 oz (30 ml)
Cherry brandy	1 oz (30 ml)
Chicken wing, quarter	1 medium
Cognac	1 oz (30 ml)
Coleslaw	4 oz (114 g)
Consommé	$\frac{1}{2}$ pt (284 ml)
Cream, sterilized	1 oz (30 ml)
Curry powder	1 oz (30 g)
Digestive biscuit, plain	1 biscuit
Drambuie	1 oz (30 ml)
Fried bread	1 oz (30 ml)
Gingernuts	1 biscuit
Grapes, black or white	4 oz (114 g)
Grapefruit, canned	4 oz (114 g)
Hovis bread	1 oz (30 g)
Jelly made with water	4 oz (114 g)
Kirsch	1 oz (30 ml)
Malt bread	1 oz (30 g)
Mincemeat	1 oz (30 g)
Minestrone soup	$\frac{1}{2}$ pt (284 ml)
Ouzo	1 oz (30 ml)
Parma ham	1 oz (30 g)
Pastilles, fruit	1 oz (30 g)
Peas, processed	3 oz (85 g)
Pernod	1 oz (30 ml)
Plums, stewed with sugar	4 oz (114 g)
Pomegranate juice, unsweetened	$\frac{1}{4}$ pt (142 ml)
Porridge	5 oz (142 g)
Prosciutto ham	1 oz (30 g)
Raisins, dried	1 oz (30 g)
Ricotta cheese	1 oz (30 g)
Rum, white or dark	1 oz (30 ml)
Rye bread, light	1 oz (30 g)
Schnapps	1 oz (30 ml)
Sherry, medium or dry	2 oz (57 ml)
Sultanas, dried	1 oz (30 g)

Vermouth, dry	2 oz (57 ml)
Vodka	1 oz (30 ml)
Wafer biscuit, filled	1 wafer
Whisky	1 oz (30 ml)
White bread	1 oz (30 g)

71–80

Advocaat	1 oz (30 ml)
Austrian cheese, smoked or with ham	1 oz (30 g)
Banana (weighed with skin)	1 medium
Bel paese cheese	1 oz (30 g)
Blackcurrants, canned in syrup	4 oz (114 g)
Cheese spread	1 portion
Cherries, stewed with sugar or canned	4 oz (114 g)
Condensed milk, skimmed sweetened	1 oz (30 ml)
Damsons, stewed with sugar	4 oz (114 g)
Egg, whole raw or boiled	1 large
Frankfurters	1 small
Jelly cubes	1 oz (30 g)
Lychees, canned	4 oz (114 g)
Milk, cows' skimmed sweetened	1 oz (30 ml)
Mussels, steamed	3 oz (85 g)
Orange juice, canned sweetened	$\frac{1}{4}$ pt (142 ml)
Paw-paw, canned	4 oz (114 g)
Peaches, stewed with sugar	4 oz (114 g)
Pears, stewed with sugar	4 oz (114 g)
Pineapple juice, canned	$\frac{1}{4}$ pt (142 ml)

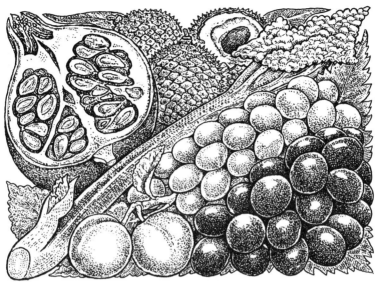

Pomegranate, raw	1 fruit
Potatoes, instant (made up)	4 oz (114 g)
Raspberries, stewed with sugar	4 oz (114 g)
Rhubarb, canned	5 oz (142 g)
Salmon, smoked	2 oz (57 g)
Shandy	½ pt (284 ml)
Sherry, sweet	2 oz (57 ml)
Sweetcorn, canned	4 oz (114 g)
Tomatoes, fried	1 medium
Tomé au raisin	1 oz (30 g)
Whelks, boiled shelled	3 oz (85 g)
Yogurt, low fat, natural	small carton

81—90

Apricots, stewed with sugar	5 oz (142 g)
Baby French cheese	1 oz (30 g)

Bengal gram, cooked (dahl)	2 oz (57 g)
Brawn	2 oz (57 g)
Brie cheese	1 oz (30 g)
Camembert cheese	1 oz (30 g)
Condensed milk, whole sweetened	1 oz (30 ml)
Crème de Cacao	1 oz (30 ml)
Crème de menthe	1 oz (30 ml)
Curaçao	1 oz (30 ml)
Edam cheese	1 oz (30 g)
Egg, poached	1 large
Golden syrup	1 tbsp
Greengages, stewed with sugar	4 oz (114 g)
Mango, canned	4 oz (114 g)
Milk, condensed sweetened	1 oz (30 ml)
Onion sauce	3 oz (85 g)
Pancakes	1 thin
Peaches, canned	4 oz (114 g)
Pears, canned	4 oz (114 g)
Peas, dried boiled	3 oz (85 g)
Pigeon peas, cooked	3 oz (85 g)
Pineapple, canned	4 oz (114 g)

Port	2 oz (57 ml)
Port Salut cheese	1 oz (30 g)
Potatoes, new boiled	4 oz (114 g)
Rye bread, dark	1 oz (30 g)
St Paulin cheese	1 oz (30 g)
Salmon, canned	2 oz (57 g)
Scallops, steamed	2 fish
Scallops, canned	3 oz (85 g)
Shredded wheat	1 oz (30 g)
Tia Maria	1 oz (30 ml)
Toast, white	1 oz (30 g)
Vermouth, sweet	2 oz (57 ml)

91—100

Apples, stewed with sugar	5 oz (142 g)
Apricots, dried stewed no sugar	5 oz (142 g)
Arrowroot	1 oz (30 g)

Baked beans in tomato sauce	5 oz (142 g)
Beer, bitter canned or draught	$\frac{1}{2}$ pt (284 ml)
Bran flakes	1 oz (30 g)
Brown ale, bottled	$\frac{1}{2}$ pt (284 ml)
Butter beans, boiled	4 oz (114 g)
Caerphilly cheese	1 oz (30 g)
Cassata	2 oz (57 g)
Chestnuts	2 oz (57 g)
Chocolate mousse, frozen	$3\frac{1}{2}$ oz (100 g)
Choux pastry, cooked	1 oz (30 g)
Cider, dry or sweet	$\frac{1}{2}$ pt (284 ml)
Coconut, fresh	1 oz (30 g)
Cointreau	1 oz (30 ml)
Cottage cheese, plain & all flavours	small carton
Crab, canned	4 oz (114 g)
Cream, whipping	1 oz (30 ml)
Danish blue cheese	1 oz (30 g)
Dolcelatte cheese	1 oz (30 g)
Double Gloucester cheese	1 oz (30 g)
Flour (all kinds)	1 oz (30 g)
Grape juice	$\frac{1}{4}$ pt (142 ml)

Grapenuts	4 oz (114 g)
Haricot beans, boiled	4 oz (114 g)
Ice cream (almost all flavours)	2 oz (57 g)
Jelly made with milk	4 oz (114 g)
Keg bitter	$\frac{1}{2}$ pt (284 ml)
Lager, bottled draught	$\frac{1}{2}$ pt (284 ml)
Lancashire cheese	1 oz (30 g)
Marshmallows	1 oz (30 g)
Mayonnaise	1 dsp
Mozzarella cheese	1 oz (30 g)
Mulberries, canned	4 oz (114 g)
Mulligatawny soup	$\frac{1}{2}$ pt (284 ml)
Onions, fried	1 oz (30 g)
Pale ale, bottled	$\frac{1}{2}$ pt (284 ml)
Pâté, chicken liver, duck and game	1 oz (30 g)
Popadom, grilled	three
Potatoes, old boiled	4 oz (114 g)
Prunes, dried stewed no sugar	4 oz (114 g)
Prunes, canned	4 oz (114 g)
Puffed wheat	1 oz (30 g)
Pumpernickel	1 oz (30 g)
Raisin bran	1 oz (30 g)
Raspberries, canned	4 oz (114 g)
Red kidney beans, cooked	4 oz (114 g)
Retsina	$\frac{1}{4}$ pt (142 ml)
Roquefort cheese	1 oz (30 g)
Sage Derby cheese	1 oz (30 g)
Sandwich biscuit	1 biscuit
Sangria	$\frac{1}{4}$ pt (142 ml)
Shortbread	1 biscuit
Soya flour, low fat	1 oz (30 g)
Spaghetti, canned in tomato sauce	6 oz (171 g)
Stout, bottled	$\frac{1}{2}$ pt (284 ml)
Sugar-coated puffed wheat	1 oz (30 g)
Sweet potatoes, boiled	4 oz (114 g)
Sweets, boiled	1 oz (30 g)
Tapioca, raw	1 oz (30 g)

Tomato sauce	4 oz (114 g)
Vegetable soup	$\frac{1}{2}$ pt (284 ml)
Wine, red, rosé, white, (not sweet), sparkling	$\frac{1}{4}$ pt (142 ml)

101—125

Abalone, steamed or canned	5 oz (142 g)
Almond paste	1 oz (30 g)
Apricots, canned	4 oz (114 g)
Apricots, dried stewed with sugar	5 oz (142 g)
Beef sausages, grilled	1 sausage
Benedictine	1 oz (30 ml)
Brain, lamb's boiled	3 oz (85 g)
Chartreuse	1 oz (30 ml)
Cheshire cheese	1 oz (30 g)
Chocolate biscuit (full coated)	1 biscuit
Cod's roe, fried	2 oz (57 g)
Cola drink	$\frac{1}{2}$ pt (284 ml)
Corned beef	2 oz (57 g)
Cornflakes	1 oz (30 g)
Cream cheese	1 oz (30 g)
Crisps, potato	small packet
Crumpet	1 crumpet
Drop scones	1 small
Emmenthal cheese	1 oz (30 g)
Fairy cake	1 small
Fruit salad, canned	4 oz (114 g)
Gooseberries, canned	4 oz (114 g)
Ham, canned	3 oz (85 g)
Hazelnuts	1 oz (30 g)
Instant porridge	1 oz (30 g)
Jam tart	1 tart
Leicester cheese	1 oz (30 g)
Lemon mousse, frozen	$3\frac{1}{2}$ oz (100 g)

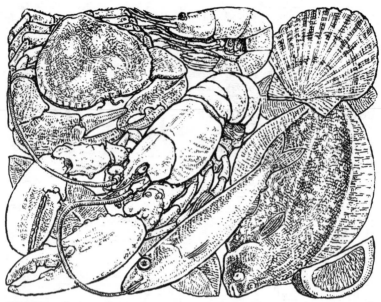

Lentils, split boiled or dahl	4 oz (114 g)
Loganberries, canned	4 oz (114 g)
Mango, raw	1 medium
Marzipan	1 oz (30 g)
Matzo biscuit	1 oz (30 g)
Mushrooms, fried	2 oz (57 g)
Oatmeal, raw	1 oz (30 g)
Octopus, steamed	5 oz (142 g)
Palm hearts, canned	4 oz (114 g)
Pâté, goose liver	1 oz (30 g)
Peanut brittle	1 oz (30 g)
Peas, split boiled	3 oz (85 g)
Peppermints	1 oz (30 g)
Pork sausages, well grilled	1 sausage
Popcorn, plain and with sugar	1 oz (30 g)
Potatoes, baked	1 small
Prunes, dried, stewed with sugar	4 oz (114 g)
Prune juice	¼ pt (142 ml)
Sardines, canned in oil or tomato sauce	2 oz (57 g)

Scallops, fried	2 fish
Scampi, boiled	3 pieces
Scotch pancakes	1 medium
Squid, steamed	5 oz (142 g)
Strawberries, canned	5 oz (142 g)
Strawberry mousse, frozen	3½ oz (100 g)
Toffees, mixed	1 oz (30 g)
Tongue, ox canned	2 oz (57 g)
Wensleydale cheese	1 oz (30 g)
White wine, sweet	¼ pt (142 ml)
Yorkshire pudding	1 small

126—150

Aubergine, fried	4 oz (114 g)
Bacon rashers, streaky grilled	2 rashers
Beef sausages, fried	1 sausage
Brain, calf's boiled	3 oz (85 g)

Chicken cream soup	½ pt (284 ml)
Cod, steamed	5 oz (142 g)
Courgette, fried	4 oz (114 g)
Crab, boiled	4 oz (114 g)
Custard, egg	4 oz (114 g)
Digestive chocolate biscuit	1 biscuit
Eccles cakes	1 small
Eggplant, fried	4 oz (114 g)
Egg, fried	1 large
Egg, scrambled	1 large
Fish cakes, fried	1 cake
Fish fingers, fried	2 fingers
Gruyère cheese	1 oz (30 g)
Haddock, steamed	5 oz (142 g)
Hake, poached	5 oz (142 g)
Herring roe, fried	2 oz (57 g)
Instant whip	5 oz (142 g)
Jellied veal	4 oz (114 g)
Lemon sole, steamed	5 oz (142 g)
Milk pudding, canned rice	6 oz (171 g)
Muffin	1 muffin
Mushroom soup, canned	½ pt (284 ml)
Oxtail soup	½ pt (284 ml)
Pilchards, canned in tomato sauce	4 oz (114 g)
Plaice, steamed	5 oz (142 g)
Plantain, green boiled	4 oz (114 g)
Popcorn, oil and salt	1 oz (30 g)
Potatoes, mashed	4 oz (114 g)
Potato rings	1 oz (30 g)
Rice pudding, canned	6 oz (171 g)
Saveloy	2 oz (57 g)
Scones, plain	1 medium
Shortcrust pastry, cooked	1 oz (30 g)
Skate, steamed	5 oz (142 g)
Soya flour, full fat	1 oz (30 g)
Stilton cheese	1 oz (30 g)
Tartare sauce	1 oz (30 g)
Tomato soup, canned	½ pt (284 ml)

Turbot, steamed	5 oz (142 g)
Walnuts, shelled	1 oz (30 g)
Whiting, steamed	5 oz (142 g)
Yogurt, flavoured	small carton
Yogurt, natural sweetened	small carton

151—175

Abalone, fried	5 oz (142 g)
Bacon rashers, back grilled	2 rashers
Béchamel sauce	4 oz (114 g)
Bran breakfast cereal	2 oz (57 g)
Cheese straws	1 oz (30 g)
Chickpeas, cooked (dahl)	4 oz (114 g)
Chicken leg quarter	1 small
Coconut, desiccated	1 oz (30 g)
Cod, fried	5 oz (142 g)
Corn-on-the-cob, boiled	1 medium
Cream, clotted	1 oz (30 ml)
Custard powder, boiled	5 oz (142 g)
Figs, stewed no sugar	5 oz (142 g)
Flaky pastry, cooked	1 oz (30 g)
Herring, pickled	2 oz (57 g)
Honeycomb	2 oz (57 g)
Lemon sponge	1 small slice
Lobster, boiled	5 oz (142 g)
Octopus, fried	5 oz (142 g)
Peanuts, fresh or salted & roasted	1 oz (30 g)
Peanut butter	1 oz (30 g)
Pistachio nuts, shelled raw	1 oz (30 g)
Polony	2 oz (57 g)
Quail, grilled or roast	1 bird
Rabbit, roast or grilled	4 oz (114 g)

Ratatouille	10 oz (284 g)
Rolls, white or brown	1 small
Scones, currant	1 medium
Skate, fried in batter	6 oz (171 g)
Sponge cake, fatless or with jam	2 oz (57 g)
Squid, fried	5 oz (142 g)
Teacakes	1 teacake
Tongue, ox boiled	2 oz (57 g)
Tuna, canned in oil (drained)	1 small can
Turkey, roast meat only	4 oz (114 g)
Vodka cocktail	3 oz (85 ml)
White sauce, savoury	4 oz (114 g)
Woodcock, roast	1 bird

Liver sausage	2 oz (57 g)
Macaroon	1 large
Pork sausages, fried	1 sausage
Potatoes, roast	2 small
Rabbit, fried or boiled	4 oz (114 g)
Scones, cheese	1 medium
Spaghetti, boiled	6 oz (171 g)
Strong ale	½ pt (284 ml)
Tagliatelle, boiled	6 oz (171 g)
Taramasalata	2 oz (57 g)
Tripe, stewed	6 oz (171 g)
Trout, steamed or smoked	1 small
Turkey, roast meat and skin	4 oz (114 g)
White sauce, sweet	4 oz (114 g)

176—200

Ackee, canned	4 oz (114 g)
Ale, strong	½ pt (284 ml)
Bacon rashers, middle grilled	2 rashers
Barley wine	½ pt (284 ml)
Bass, steamed	5 oz (142 g)
Beef, silverside boiled (lean only)	4 oz (114 g)
Blancmange	6 oz (171 g)
Bream, steamed	5 oz (142 g)
Carp, steamed	5 oz (142 g)
Dumpling, suet	1 medium
Figs, stewed with sugar	5 oz (142 g)
French dressing	1 oz (30 ml)
Glucose drink	½ pt (28 ml)
Halibut, steamed or poached	5 oz (142 g)
Ham, smoked	3 oz (85 g)
Houmous	2 oz (57 g)
Irish coffee	¼ pt (142 ml)
Kidney, lamb's fried	4 oz (114 g)

201—250

Avocado pear	½ large
Bacon rashers, streaky fried	2 rashers
Bass, fried	5 oz (142 g)
Beef, sirloin roast	3 oz (85 g)
Bloody Mary	7 oz (199 ml)
Bolognese sauce	6 oz (171 g)
Bream, fried	5 oz (142 g)
Brioche	1 roll
Carp, fried	5 oz (142 g)
Chicken, boiled light meat	5 oz (142 g)
Chicken, roast meat only	5 oz (142 g)
Chocolate, milk or plain	small bar
Cream, single	small carton
Danish pastry (apricot filling)	1 small
Eclairs	1 small
Eel, jellied	4 oz (114 g)
Fancy iced cakes	1 small

Haddock, fried	5 oz (142 g)
Halibut, fried	5 oz (142 g)
Ham, boiled	3 oz (85 g)
Ham and pork, canned	3 oz (85 g)
Hare, roast	4 oz (114 g)
Lamb cutlet, grilled	1 cutlet
Liver, chicken fried	4 oz (114 g)
Milk pudding	6 oz (171 g)
Mince pies	1 pie
Muesli	2 oz (57 g)
Mullet, steamed	5 oz (142 g)
Partridge, roast	4 oz (114 g)
Pheasant, roast	4 oz (114 g)
Pilchards, canned in oil	4 oz (114 g)
Rice pudding	6 oz (171 g)
Sago pudding	6 oz (171 g)
Sausage roll, short pastry	1 small
Screw driver	¼ pt (142 ml)
Semolina pudding	6 oz (171 g)
Shrimps, potted	2 oz (57 g)

Suet, shredded	1 oz (30 g)
Tapioca pudding	4 oz (114 g)
Tom Collins	½ pt (284 ml)
Turbot, fried in breadcrumbs	5 oz (142 g)
Venison, roast, fried or grilled	4 oz (114 g)
Whisky sour	4½ oz (128 ml)
Yam, boiled	6 oz (171 g)

251—300

Apple pie	6 oz (171 g)
Bacon, gammon joint boiled or rashers grilled	4 oz (114 g)
Bacon rashers, fried back or middle	2 rashers

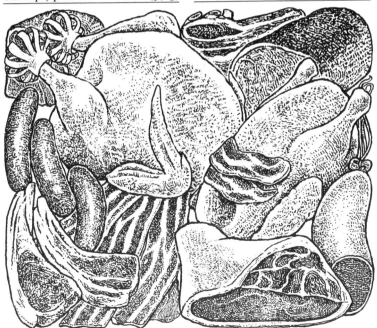

Beef, mince stewed	4 oz (114 g)	Fish pie	8 oz (227 g)
Beef, silverside boiled	4 oz (114 g)	French onion soup	½ pt (284 ml)
Beef, stewing steak, cooked	4 oz (114 g)	Frogs' legs, fried in batter	12 legs
Beefburgers, fried or grilled	1 average	Fruit cakes, rich, iced or plain	3 oz (85 g)
Cauliflower cheese	8 oz (227 g)	Grouse, roast	1 small
Chapati, fatless	1 large	Heart, sheep's roast	4 oz (114 g)
Cheese pudding	6 oz (171 g)	Heart, ox stewed	6 oz (171 g)
Cheese sauce	5 oz (142 g)	Herring, steamed	5 oz (142 g)
Chicken, boiled meat only	5 oz (142 g)	Kedgeree	7 oz (199 g)
Chicken, boiled dark meat	5 oz (142 g)	Kidney, ox stewed	6 oz (171 g)
Chicken, roast meat and skin	5 oz (142 g)	Kidney, pig's stewed	6 oz (171 g)
		Kipper, baked	5 oz (142 g)
Cider, vintage	½ pt (284 ml)	Lamb, leg roast	4 oz (114 g)
Coconut oil	1 oz (30 ml)	Lard	1 oz (30 g)
Corn oil	1 oz (30 ml)	Lentil soup	½ pt (284 ml)
Croissant	1 croissant	Liver, calf's fried	4 oz (114 g)
Curried meat	6 oz (171 g)	Liver, lamb's fried	4 oz (114 g)
Dripping, beef	1 oz (30 g)	Luncheon meat, canned	3 oz (85 g)
Duck, roast meat only	5 oz (142 g)	Mackerel, fried	5 oz (142 g)
Eel, steamed	5 oz (142 g)	Maize oil	1 oz (30 ml)
		Mortadella	3 oz (85 g)

Mullet, fried	5 oz (142 g)
Olive oil	1 oz (30 ml)
Omelette, plain	5 oz (142 g)
Palm oil	1 oz (30 ml)
Peanut oil	1 oz (30 ml)
Pigeon, roast	4 oz (114 g)
Pizza, cheese and tomato	1 small
Plantain, ripe fried	4 oz (114 g)
Plum pie	6 oz (171 g)
Rabbit, stewed	6 oz (171 g)
Rhubarb pie	6 oz (171 g)
Rollmops	4 oz (114 g)
Safflower oil	1 oz (30 ml)
Salami	2 oz (57 g)
Salmon, steamed	5 oz (142 g)
Salmon trout, poached	5 oz (142 g)
Sausage roll, flaky pastry	1 small
Scampi, fried in batter	3 pieces
Skate, fried in breadcrumbs	6 oz (171 g)
Snails, with butter	6 snails
Soya oil	1 oz (30 ml)
Sponge cake, with fat	2 oz (57 g)
Squid, fried in batter	5 oz (142 g)
Suet, block	1 oz (30 g)
Sultana cake	3 oz (85 g)
Sunflower oil	1 oz (30 ml)
Sweetbread, lamb fried	4 oz (114 g)
Swiss roll	4 oz (114 g)
Veal, roast	4 oz (114 g)
White pudding	2 oz (57 g)
Whiting, fried	5 oz (142 g)

Black pudding, fried	4 oz (114 g)
Brazil nuts	2 oz (57 g)
Christmas pudding	4 oz (114 g)
Cod, fried in batter or breadcrumbs	6 oz (171 g)
Currant bun	1 bun
Date and walnut loaf	4 oz (114 g)
Eel, fried in batter	6 oz (171 g)
Eel, smoked	2 oz (57 g)
Gingerbread	3 oz (85 g)
Hare, stewed	6 oz (171 g)
Herring, fried in oatmeal	5 oz (142 g)
Hot cross bun	1 bun
Hot pot	10 oz (284 g)
Kipper, fried	5 oz (142 g)
Lamb, scrag and neck stewed	5 oz (142 g)
Lemon sole, fried in breadcrumbs	5 oz (142 g)
Liquorice allsorts	4 oz (114 g)
Liver, ox stewed	6 oz (171 g)
Liver, pig's stewed	6 oz (171 g)
Macaroni, boiled	10 oz (284 g)
Madeira cake	3 oz (85 g)
Octopus, fried in batter	5 oz (142 g)
Plaice, fried in breadcrumbs	5 oz (142 g)
Pork, leg roast	4 oz (114 g)
Salmon, fried	5 oz (142 g)
Shepherd's pie	10 oz (284 g)
Trout, fried	1 small

301—350

Almonds	2 oz (57 g)
Beef steak, grilled	6 oz (171 g) (weighed raw)
Beef stew	10 oz (284 g)

351—400

Beef, brisket boiled	4 oz (114 g)
Beef, forerib roast	4 oz (114 g)
Beef, steak fried	6 oz (171 g) (weighed raw)

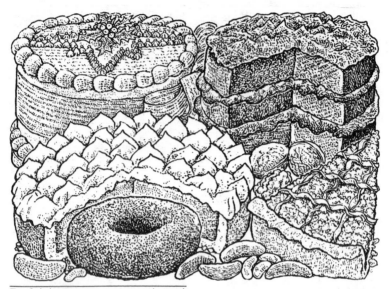

Beef, joint roast	4 oz (114 g)
Beef, steak pudding	6 oz (171 g)
Cheese soufflé	5 oz (142 g)
Chelsea bun	1 bun
Christmas cake	4 oz (114 g)
Currant bun, iced	1 bun
Custard tart	4 oz (114 g)
Dogfish, fried in batter	5 oz (142 g)
Dundee cake	4 oz (114 g)
Goose, roast	4 oz (114 g)
Lamb, chop grilled	4 oz (114 g)
Lamb, shoulder roast	4 oz (114 g)
Lemon meringue pie	4 oz (114 g)
Mackerel, steamed	5 oz (142 g)
Plaice, fried in batter	5 oz (142 g)
Queen of puddings	6 oz (171 g)
Ravioli	6 oz (171 g)
Rock salmon, fried in batter	5 oz (142 g)
Sponge pudding	4 oz (114 g)
Stewed steak with gravy	8 oz (227 g)
Trifle	6 oz (171 g)
Veal cutlet, fried	1 cutlet

401—450

Bloater, grilled	6 oz (171 g)
Cheesecake, plain or currant	4 oz (114 g)
Chilli con carne	12 oz (341 g)
Chips, fresh potato	6 oz (171 g)
Doughnuts, plain or with jam	1 doughnut
Lardy cake	4 oz (114 g)
Mackerel, smoked	5 oz (142 g)
Pork, belly rashers grilled	4 oz (114 g)
Pork pie	4 oz (114 g)
Quail, fried	1 bird
Quiche Lorraine	1 small slice
Rock bun	1 bun
Scampi, fried in breadcrumbs	3 pieces
Simnel cake	4 oz (114 g)
Treacle tart	4 oz (114 g)
Welsh rarebit	4 oz (114 g)

451—500

Apple crumble	8 oz (227 g)
Chapati, with fat	1 large
Chips, frozen fried	6 oz (171 g)
Lamb, breast roast	4 oz (114 g)
Macaroni cheese	10 oz (284 g)
Sprats, fried or fried in batter	4 oz (114 g)
Suet pudding, steamed	5 oz (142 g)
Tongue, sheep stewed	6 oz (171 g)

501—600

Chocolate fancy	4 oz (114 g)
Cornish pasty	6 oz (171 g)
Cream, double	small carton

Faggots	2 faggots
Haggis, boiled	6 oz (171 g)
Irish stew	15 oz (426 g)
Moussaka	10 oz (284 g)
Oxtail, stewed	8 oz (227 g)
Pork, chop grilled	1 chop
Scotch egg	1 egg
Whitebait, fried, in batter or in flour	4 oz (114 g)

601—700

Cashew nuts	4 oz (114 g)
Pork pie	1 in (3 cm) slice
Steak and kidney pie	8 oz (227 g)
Steak pie	individual

CARBOHYDRATE UNIT GROUPS

¼

Asparagus	4 oz (114 g)
Bamboo shoots, canned	1 oz (30 g)
Coconut, fresh	1 oz (30 g)
Cream, sterilized	1 oz (30 ml)
Frankfurter	1 small
Lemon curd, homemade	1 tsp
Milk	1 oz (30 ml)
Piccalilli	1 oz (30 g)
Quince, raw	1 oz (30 g)
Walnuts	1 oz (30 g)

½

Almonds	2 oz (57 g)
Apricot, fresh	1 medium
Artichoke, globe	1 medium
Artichoke hearts, boiled or canned	4 oz (114 g)
Avocado pear	½ large
Brazil nuts	2 oz (57 g)
Brown sauce (bottled)	1 tsp
Cheese footballs	1
Clementine	1 small

Coconut milk	2 oz (57 ml)
Coffee/Chicory essence	1 tsp
Courgettes, fried	4 oz (114 g)
Cranberries, raw	1 oz (30 g)
Crispbread, starch-reduced	1 biscuit
Dried milk, whole or skimmed	1 tsp
Herring roe, fried	2 oz (57 g)
Houmous	2 oz (57 g)
Ladies fingers (okra), boiled or canned	4 oz (114 g)
Lemon curd (in jar)	1 tsp
Lemon sole, fried in breadcrumbs	5 oz (142 g)
Liver sausage	2 oz (57 g)
Onion, fried	1 oz (30 g)
Peanuts	1 oz (30 g)

Plum, fresh	1 medium
Salad cream	1 dsp
Twiglets	1

³/₄

Evaporated milk	1 oz (30 ml)
Gooseberries, raw or stewed no sugar	4 oz (114 g)
Honey	1 tsp
Horseradish sauce	1 dsp
Peanut butter	1 oz (30 g)
Suet, shredded	1 oz (30 g)
Tomato purée	1 oz (30 g)
Turnips, boiled	6 oz (171 g)

1

Aubergine, fried	4 oz (114 g)
Beefburger, grilled	1 average
Black pudding	2 oz (57 g)
Blackberries, blackcurrants, raw or stewed no sugar	4oz (114 g)
Bolognese sauce	6 oz (171 g)
Buttermilk	$\frac{1}{4}$ pt (142 ml)
Carrots	4 oz (114 g)
Coleslaw	4 oz (114 g)
Cottage cheese and pineapple	1 small carton
Cornflour	1 tsp
Cranberry sauce	1 dsp
Cream, single	1 small carton
Crispbread, rye or wheat	1 biscuit
Figs, fresh	1 fig
Glucose	1 tsp
Greengages	1 fruit
Grissini	1
Jerusalem artichokes, boiled	4 oz (114 g)
Jam (all kinds)	1 tsp
Liver, chicken or lamb, fried	4 oz (114 g)
Liver, ox or pig, stewed	4 oz (114 g)
Luncheon meat	3 oz (85 g)
Lychees, fresh	1 oz (30 g)
Malted milk powder	2 tsp
Mandarin	1 small
Marmalade	1 tsp
Melon, honeydew	1 medium slice
Melon, ogen	$\frac{1}{2}$ medium
Palmier	1 biscuit
Peas, fresh or frozen boiled	3 oz (85 g)
Plums, cooking, raw or stewed no sugar	4 oz (114 g)
Pistachio nuts, shelled	1 oz (30 g)

Raspberries, raw or stewed no sugar	4 oz (114 g)
Redcurrants, raw or stewed no sugar	4 oz (114 g)
Rosehip syrup	1 tsp
Satsuma	1 medium
Sausages, pork or beef, fried or grilled	1 sausage
Saveloy	2 oz (57 g)
Sauerkraut	4 oz (114 g)
Skate, fried in breadcrumbs	6 oz (171 g)
Soya beans, cooked	4 oz (114 g)
Sugar	1 tsp
Sweetbreads, fried	4 oz (114 g)
Tangerine	1 medium
Taramasalata	2 oz (57 g)
Tomato juice	$\frac{1}{4}$ pt (142 ml)
Tomato ketchup	1 oz (30 g)
Tonic water	4 oz (114 ml)
Turbot, fried in breadcrumbs	5 oz (142 g)
Whitebait, fried in flour	4 oz (114 g)
Whitecurrants, raw or stewed no sugar	4 oz (114 g)
Yogurt, natural	1 small carton

1½

Apple, eating or cooking	1 medium
Biscuits, bourbon, butter, coconut, custard cream, fruit shortcake	1 biscuit
Bread sauce	2 oz (57 g)
Cheese straws	1 oz (30 g)
Chocolate, drinking	2 tsp
Choux pastry	1 oz (30 g)
Coconut, desiccated	1 oz (30 g)
Cod's roe, fried	2 oz (57 g)

Cream crackers	1 cracker
Curry powder	1 oz (30 g)
Dogfish, fried in batter	5 oz (142 g)
Eel, fried in batter	6 oz (171 g)
Lentils, cooked	4 oz (114 g)
Lime juice, undiluted	1 oz (30 ml)
Madeira	1 oz (30 g)
Mint sauce, in jars, undiluted	1 oz (30 g)
Mung beans, cooked	4 oz (114 g)
Orange or Lemon squash, undiluted	1 oz (30 ml)
Passion fruit, raw	4 oz (114 g)
Semi-sweet biscuit	1 biscuit
Soya flour (full fat)	1 oz (30 g)
Veal cutlet, fried	1 medium
Wafer biscuit, filled	1 biscuit

2

Béchamel sauce	4 oz (114 g)
Beef stew	10 oz (284 g)
Bengal gram, cooked – dahl	2 oz (57 g)
Bitter lemon	4 oz (114 ml)
Black treacle	1 tbsp
Broad beans, boiled	4 oz (114 g)
Carrot juice	$\frac{1}{4}$ pt (142 ml)
Cauliflower cheese	8 oz (227 g)
Cheese sauce	4 oz (114 g)
Cherries, raw or stewed no sugar	4 oz (114 g)
Chicken noodle soup	$\frac{1}{2}$ pt (284 ml)
Chicken, cream soup	$\frac{1}{2}$ pt (284 ml)
Chocolate-covered sponge biscuit	1 biscuit
Cod, fried in batter	6 oz (171 g)
Damsons, raw or stewed no sugar	4 oz (114 g)

Flaked wheat biscuits	1 biscuit
Gooseberries, ripe raw	4 oz (114 g)
Ginger ale	4 oz (114 ml)
Gingernuts	1 biscuit
Grapefruit	$\frac{1}{2}$ medium
Grapefruit juice	$\frac{1}{4}$ pt (142 ml)
Greengages, stewed no sugar	4 oz (114 g)
High protein corn flakes	$\frac{1}{2}$ oz (14 g)
Ice cream, non-dairy	2 oz (57 g)
Melon, cantaloupe	1 medium slice
Minestrone soup	$\frac{1}{2}$ pt (284 ml)
Mulberries, raw	4 oz (114 g)
Mushroom soup	$\frac{1}{2}$ pt (284 ml)
Oatcakes	1 biscuit
Orange, segments	4 oz (114 g)
Orange, whole	1 large
Oxtail soup	$\frac{1}{2}$ pt (284 ml)
Oxtail stew	8 oz (227 g)
Peach, raw or stewed no sugar	1 large
Pearl barley, boiled	1 oz (30 g)
Pears, eating or cooking raw	1 small
Pears, stewed no sugar	4 oz (114 g)
Porridge	4 oz (114 g)
Prunes, dry raw	1 oz (30 g)
Rock salmon, fried in batter	5 oz (142 g)
Scampi, fried in batter	3 pieces
Soya flour, low fat	1 oz (30 g)
Sprats, fried in batter	4 oz (114 g)
Squid, fried in batter	5 oz (142 g)
Strawberries, raw	6 oz (171 g)
Tomato chutney	1 oz (30 g)
Water biscuit	1 biscuit
Whitebait, fried in batter	4 oz (114 g)
White sauce, savoury	4 oz (114 g)
sweet	2 oz (57 g)
Whiting, fried	5 oz (142 g)

2½

Apples, stewed no sugar	5 oz (142 g)
Apricots, dried	1 oz (30 g)
Biscuits, sandwich	1 biscuit
Bread, brown, hovis or wholemeal	1 oz (30 g)
Cheese sauce	5 oz (142 g)
Crisped rice breakfast cereal	½ oz (14 g)
Crisps	1 small pkt
Dahl (lentils)	4 oz (114 g)
Egg custard	4 oz (114 g)
Figs, dried	1 fig
Flaky pastry	1 oz (30 g)
Fruit gums	1 oz (30 g)
Meringue	1 large
Milk chocolate and brazil nuts	1 oz (30 g)
Milk chocolate covered wafer biscuit	2 fingers
Octopus, fried in batter	5 oz (142 g)

Orange juice, unsweetened	¼ pt (142 ml)
Shortbread	1 biscuit
Strawberry mousse, frozen	3½ oz (100 g)

3

Advocaat	1 oz (30 ml)
Anisette	1 oz (30 ml)
Apple chutney	1 oz (30 g)
Armagnac	1 oz (30 ml)
Baked beans in tomato sauce	5 oz (142 g)
Banana	1 medium
Beer, draught, mild	½ pt (284 ml)
Bilberries	4 oz (114 g)
Blackcurrant liqueur	1 oz (30 ml)
Bourbon	1 oz (30 ml)
Brown ale, bottled	½ pt (284 ml)
Calvados	1 oz (30 ml)
Cassis	1 oz (30 ml)
Cheese pudding	6 oz (171 g)

Cheese soufflé	5 oz (142 g)	Malt loaf	1 oz (30 g)
Chocolate mousse, frozen	3½ oz (100 g)	Marzipan	1 oz (30 g)
Cherry brandy	1 oz (30 ml)	Milk chocolate + fruit and nuts	1 oz (30 g)
Condensed milk, sweetened	1 oz (30 ml)	Milk chocolate, wholenut	1 oz (30 g)
Cognac	1 oz (30 ml)	Milk chocolate coated coconut bar	1 oz (30 g)
Crème de Cacao	1 oz (30 ml)	Mulligatawny soup	½ pt (284 ml)
Crème de menthe	1 oz (30 ml)	Ouzo	1 oz (30 ml)
Crumpets	1 crumpet	Parsnips, boiled	4 oz (114 g)
Curaçao	1 oz (30 ml)	Peaches, dried raw	1 oz (30 g)
Drambuie	1 oz (30 ml)	Peas, processed	1 oz (30 g)
Drop scones	1 small	Peas, dried boiled	3 oz (85 g)
Fried bread	1 oz (30 g)	Peas, pigeon	3 oz (85 g)
Gin	1 oz (30 ml)	Pineapple, fresh	4 oz (114 g)
Gooseberries, stewed with sugar	4 oz (114 g)	Plain chocolate and almonds	1 oz (30 g)
Grand Marnier	1 oz (30 ml)	Pomegranate juice	¼ pt (142 ml)
Ice cream, dairy (all kinds)	2 oz (57 g)	Popcorn with oil and salt	1 oz (30 g)
Jelly, made up	4 oz (114 g)	Potatoes, new canned	4 oz (114 g)
Kirsch	1 oz (30 ml)	Redcurrants, stewed with sugar	4 oz (114 g)
Lager, draught or bottled	½ pt (284 ml)	Rhubarb, canned or stewed with sugar	5 oz (142 g)
Lemonade	½ pt (284 ml)	Rum, dark or light	1 oz (30 ml)
Loganberries, stewed with sugar	4 oz (114 g)		

Rye bread, light	1 oz (30 g)
Scotch pancake	1 medium
Schnapps	1 oz (30 ml)
Sherry, dry	2 oz (57 ml)
Shortcrust pastry	1 oz (30 g)
Skate, fried in batter	6 oz (171 g)
Tangerines, canned	4 oz (114 g)
Tomato soup, canned	½ pt (284 ml)
Tia Maria	1 oz (30 ml)
Vodka	1 oz (30 ml)
Watermelon	1 large slice
Whisky	1 oz (30 ml)
Whitecurrants, stewed with sugar	4 oz (114 g)
Yorkshire pudding	1 small

Fairy cake	1 small
Flour, wholemeal	1 oz (30 g)
Fruit pastilles	1 oz (30 g)
Grapefruit, canned in syrup	4 oz (114 g)
Jam tart	1 tart
Jelly cubes	1 oz (30 g)
Kedgeree	7 oz (199 g)
Liquorice gums	1 oz (30 g)
Milk chocolate	1 oz (30 g)
Milk chocolate covered fudge	1 finger
Plain chocolate	1 oz (30 g)
Potato rings	1 oz (30 g)
Raisins or sultanas	1 oz (30 g)
Sherry, medium	2 oz (57 ml)
Toast, white	1 oz (30 g)

3½

Apple, dried	1 oz (30 g)
Apple juice, natural	¼ pt (142 ml)
Baked apple and sugar	6 oz (171 g)
Black pudding, fried	4 oz (114 g)
Black rye bread (pumpernickel)	1 oz (30 g)
Blackberries, canned or stewed with sugar	4 oz (114 g)
Blackcurrants, stewed with sugar	4 oz (114 g)
Blackcurrant juice, undiluted	1 oz (30 ml)
Cashew nuts	4 oz (114 g)
Chocolate biscuits	1 biscuit
Chocolate covered toffees	1 oz (30 g)
Condensed milk, skimmed sweetened	1 oz (30 ml)

4

Butter beans, boiled	4 oz (114 g)
Champagne	4 oz (114 ml)
Chartreuse	1 oz (30 ml)
Cherries, canned or stewed with sugar	4 oz (114 g)
Chestnuts	2 oz (57 g)
Chickpeas (dahl)	4 oz (114 g)
Chilli con carne	12 oz (341 g)
Cointreau	1 oz (30 ml)
Damsons, stewed with sugar	4 oz (114 g)
Eccles cake	1 small
Eclair	1 small
Flour, brown or white	1 oz (30 g)
French onion soup	½ pt (284 ml)
Grapes, black or white	4 oz (114 g)
Greengages, stewed with sugar	4 oz (114 g)

Guavas, canned	4 oz (114 g)	Potatoes, old boiled	4 oz (114 g)
Haricot beans, boiled	4 oz (114 g)	Potatoes, old mashed	4 oz (114 g)
Instant porridge	1 oz (30 g)	Potatoes, new boiled	4 oz (114 g)
Lentils, boiled	4 oz (114 g)	Prunes, stewed no sugar	4 oz (114 g)
Liquorice, allsorts or stick	1 oz (30 g)	Puffed wheat	1 oz (30 g)
Lychees, canned	4 oz (114 g)	Quiche Lorraine	1 small slice
Mandarins, canned	4 oz (114 g)	Raspberries, stewed with sugar	4 oz (114 g)
Mango, canned	4 oz (114 g)	Red kidney beans, cooked	4 oz (114 g)
Milk jelly	4 oz (114 g)	Sausage roll	1 small
Mints, after dinner	1 oz (30 g)	Scone, plain	1 medium
Mulberries, canned	4 oz (114 g)	Scotch egg	1 egg
Oatmeal, raw	1 oz (30 g)	Shandy	½ pt (284 ml)
Paw-paw, canned	4 oz (114 g)	Sherry, sweet	2 oz (57 ml)
Peaches, canned or stewed with sugar	4 oz (114 g)	Shredded wheat	1 oz (30 g)
Peanut brittle	1 oz (30 g)	Spaghetti in tomato sauce	6 oz (171 g)
Pears, canned or stewed with sugar	4 oz (114 g)	Sweetcorn, canned	4 oz (114 g)
Peas, split boiled	3 oz (85 g)	Sweet potato, boiled	4 oz (114 g)
Pineapple, canned	4 oz (114 g)	Tapioca pudding	4 oz (114 g)
Pineapple juice	¼ pt (142 ml)	Toffees, mixed	1 oz (30 g)
Plaice, fried in batter	5 oz (142 g)	Vegetable soup, canned or packet	½ pt (284 ml)
Plums, stewed with sugar	4 oz (114 g)	Vermouth, dry	2 oz (57 ml)
Pomegranate	1 fruit	White pudding	2 oz (57 g)
Popadom, grilled	three	White sauce, savoury	4 oz (114 g)
Popcorn, plain	1 oz (30 g)	Yogurt, flavoured	1 small carton
Port	2 oz (57 ml)		

4½

Bran flakes	1 oz (30 g)
Breadcrumbs, dried	1 oz (30 g)
Cheesecake, plain	4 oz (114 g)
Cheese scone	1 medium
Fudge	1 oz (30 g)
Golden syrup	1 tbsp
Grapenuts	1 oz (30 g)
Instant whip	5 oz (142 g)
Marshmallows	1 oz (30 g)
Raisin bran	1 oz (30 g)
Rye flour	1 oz (30 g)
Suet dumpling	1 medium
Welsh rarebit	4 oz (114 g)
Yogurt, sweetened natural	1 small carton

Cola drink	½ pt (284 ml)
Cornflakes	1 oz (30 g)
Custard, made up	¼ pt (142 ml)
Ice cream cornet	1 cornet
Irish coffee	¼ pt (142 ml)
Keg bitter	½ pt (284 ml)
Matzo biscuit	1 biscuit
Moussaka	10 oz (284 g)
Popcorn and sugar	1 oz (30 g)
Prune juice	¼ pt (142 ml)
Raspberries, canned	4 oz (114 g)
Retsina	¼ pt (142 ml)
Rice pudding, canned	6 oz (171 g)
Sangria	¼ pt (142 ml)
Semolina pudding	6 oz (171 g)
Shepherd's pie	10 oz (284 g)
Strawberries, canned	5 oz (142 g)
Sugar-coated puffed wheat	1 oz (30 g)
Tagliatelle, raw	1 oz (30 g)
Vermouth, sweet	2 oz (57 ml)
Wine, red, rosé, white dry, medium or sparkling	¼ pt (142 ml)
Yogurt, fruit or hazelnut	1 small carton

5

Apples, stewed with sugar	5 oz (142 g)
Beer, canned or draught bitter	½ pt (284 ml)
Benedictine	1 oz (30 ml)
Blackcurrants, canned in syrup	4 oz (114 g)
Boiled sweets	1 oz (30 g)
Bran breakfast cereal	2 oz (57 g)
Bread roll, brown soft	1 small
Brioche	1 brioche
Brown ale, bottled	½ pt (284 ml)
Cheesecake, currant	4 oz (114 g)
Cider, dry or sweet	½ pt (284 ml)

5½

Arrowroot	1 oz (30 g)
Milk chocolate covered caramel bar	2 oz (57 g) bar
caramel and nuts	1½ oz (43 g) bar
Muffin	1 average
Orange juice, sweetened	¼ pt (142 ml)
Peppermint creams	1 oz (30 g)

6

Apple sauce	2 oz (57 g)
Apricots, canned or stewed with sugar	4 oz (114 g)
Bread roll, brown crusty or white soft	1 small
Corn-on-the-cob, boiled	1 medium
Chocolate-covered cream egg	1 egg
Croissant	1 croissant
Dates, dried	2 oz (57 g)
Fish pie	8 oz (227 g)
Fruit salad, canned	4 oz (114 g)
Hot-pot	10 oz (284 g)
Lemon sponge cake	1 small slice
Lentil soup	6 oz (171 ml)
Loganberries, canned	4 oz (114 g)
Mango	1 medium
Mince pie	1 pie
Palm hearts, canned	4 oz (114 g)
Peppermints	1 oz (30 g)
Pizza	1 small
Pork pie	4 oz (114 g)
Potatoes, baked	1 small
Potatoes, roast	2 small
Prunes, canned or stewed with sugar	4 oz (114 g)
Rice pudding	6 oz (171 g)
Sago pudding	6 oz (171 g)
Sponge cake	1 small slice
Teacakes	1 cake
Vodka cocktail	3 oz (85 ml)

6½

Apple strudel	4 oz (114 g)
Blancmange	6 oz (171 g)

7

Apricots, stewed with sugar	5 oz (142 g)
Bread roll, white crusty	1 small
Cherry cake	4 oz (114 g)
Custard tart	4 oz (114 g)
Faggots	2 faggots
Jam sponge	1 small slice
Plantain, green boiled or ripe fried	4 oz (114 g)
Trifle	6 oz (171 g)
White wine, sweet	¼ pt (142 ml)

7½

Fruit pies, apple, plum, rhubarb or gooseberry	6 oz (171 g)

8

Cakes, small iced	1 cake
Figs, stewed no sugar	5 oz (142 g)
Honeycomb	2 oz (57 g)
Muesli	2 oz (57 g)
Ravioli	6 oz (171 g)
Scampi, fried in breadcrumbs	3 pieces
Steak and kidney pie, single crust	8 oz (227 g)
Tom Collins	½ pt (284 ml)

9

Bloody Mary	7 oz (199 ml)
Doughnut	1 average
Fruit cake, plain or rich	3 oz (85 g)
Grape juice	½ pt (284 ml)
Irish stew	15 oz (426 g)
Sultana cake	3 oz (85 g)
Spaghetti, boiled	6 oz (171 g)
Tagliatelle, boiled	6 oz (171 g)

10

Barley wine	½ pt (284 ml)
Brown ale, strong	½ pt (284 ml)
Chips, frozen fried	6 oz (171 g)
Cider, vintage	½ pt (284 ml)
Figs, stewed with sugar	5 oz (142 g)
Fruit cake, iced	3 oz (85 g)
Glucose drink	½ pt (284 ml)
Hot cross bun	1 average
Lemon meringue pie	4 oz (114 g)
Macaroni cheese	10 oz (284 g)

Madeira cake	3 oz (85 g)
Screwdriver	¼ pt (142 ml)
Sponge pudding	4 oz (114 g)
Yam, boiled	6 oz (171 g)

The following items have *more* than 10 carbohydrate units per portion. Check the main tables for the actual values.

11–15

Angel cake	4 oz (114 g)
Christmas cake	4 oz (114 g)
Chapati	1 large
Chelsea bun	1 bun
Chips, fresh fried	6 oz (171 g)
Chocolates, fancy	4 oz (114 g)
Cornish pasty	6 oz (171 g)
Currant buns	1 bun
Date and walnut loaf	4 oz (114 g)
Doughnut with jam	1 doughnut
Dundee cake	4 oz (114 g)
Lardy cake	4 oz (114 g)
Liquorice allsorts	4 oz (114 g)
Simnel cake	4 oz (114 g)
Steak and kidney pie, individual	8 oz (227 g)
Steamed suet pudding	5 oz (142 g)
Swiss roll	4 oz (114 g)
Treacle tart	4 oz (114 g)
Whisky sour	4½ oz (128 ml)

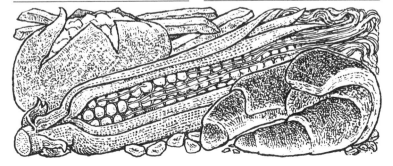

TABLE 3

This section gives Calorie and carbohydrate values for dishes which may be commonly eaten, either at home or when out for a meal. These values are obviously for guidance only as they have been calculated from specific recipes. They will, however give you some idea of which items would do the least or greatest 'damage' to your controlled diet.

	Size of average portion	Calories per portion	Carbohydrate units per portion

BREAKFAST

Boiled egg	1 large	80	—
Cereals + milk	small bowl		
+ sugar	2 tsp	130	5
Coddled egg	1 large	120	—
Coffee			
black	5 oz (142 ml)	0	0
+ milk only	1 oz (30 ml)	20	$\frac{1}{4}$
+ milk & sugar	2 tsp	60	$2\frac{1}{4}$
Croissant + butter	1 croissant	320	6
Fried bacon	1 back rasher		
+ fried egg	+ 1 large	260	—
Fried liver + bacon	2 oz (57 g) + 1 back rasher	220	—
Fried pork sausage	1 sausage		
+ fried egg	+ 1 large	310	1
Fruit juice	$\frac{1}{4}$ pt (142 ml)	50	$2\frac{1}{2}$
Grapefruit + sugar	$\frac{1}{2}$ medium + 1 tsp	45	5
Grilled kidneys	4 oz (114 g)		
+ fried bread	+ 1 slice	260	3
Grilled kipper	5 oz (142 g)	290	—
Grilled sausage	1 sausage		
+ grilled tomatoes	+ 2 medium	210	1
Grilled tomatoes	2 medium		
on toast	1 slice*	140	3

* calculated as one thin slice of cut bread + a scraping of butter

	Size of average portion	Calories per portion	Carbohydrate units per portion
Kedgeree	7 oz (199 g)	300	$3\frac{1}{2}$
Muesli	2 tbsp	210	8
Mushrooms	2 oz (57 g)		
on toast	1 slice★	115	3
Poached egg	1 large	90	—
on toast	1 slice★	200	3
Porridge	small bowl	65	2
+ sugar	2 tsp	85	4
Sardines in tomato sauce	3 oz (85 g)		
on toast	1 slice★	260	3
Scrambled egg			
on toast	1 slice★	250	3
Tea + milk	5 oz (142 ml) + 1 oz (30 g)	20	$\frac{1}{4}$
+ sugar	2 tsp	60	$2\frac{1}{4}$
Toast + butter	1 slice★	110	3
+ marmalade	2 tsp	150	5

LUNCH (main courses)

Beef curry	12 oz (341 g)	500	2
Boiled beef & dumpling	14 oz (397 g)	790	5
Cauliflower cheese	8 oz (227 g)	255	2
Cheese & potato pie	8 oz (227 g)	370	6
Cheese & onion pie	4 oz (114 g)	460	8

★ calculated as one thin slice of cut bread + a scraping of butter

	Size of average portion	Calories per portion	Carbohydrate units per portion
Chicken casserole	18 oz (511 g)	410	1
Chicken paprika	18 oz (511 g)	830	4
Chicken pie (puff pastry)	8 oz (227 g)	400	4
Chicken risotto	14 oz (397 g)	500	13
Coleslaw	4 oz (114 g)	70	1
Coq au vin	20 oz (567 g)	620	3
Cornish pasty	1 small	570	11
Cream of vegetable soup	$\frac{1}{2}$ pt (284 ml)	150	2
Fish cakes	2 cakes	260	4
Fish & chips	7 oz (199 g)+ 5 oz (142 g)	750	16
Fish pie (fish in white sauce and potato topping)	10 oz (284 g)	350	7
French onion soup (with bread and cheese)	14 oz (397 g)	370	6
Gammon and pineapple	7 oz (199 g)	300	2
Green salad (French dressing)	4 oz (114 g)	150	—
Grilled lamb chops	2 small	600	—
Grilled pork chops	1 large	565	—
Hamburger plain	$\frac{1}{4}$ lb (114 g)	230	1
+ roll (soft)	2 oz (57 g)	400	7
+ cheese	1 oz (30 g)	490	7
Lancashire hot pot (chops + veg. + sliced potatoes + gravy)	16 oz (454 g)	570	8
Meat loaf	6 oz (171 g)	370	3

	Size of average portion	Calories per portion	Carbohydrate units per portion
Minestrone soup	½ pt (284 ml)	65	2
Mixed salad (lettuce, cauliflower, avocado, tomato, cress, and almonds)	4 oz (114 g)	120	—
Onions in white sauce	5 oz (142 g)	160	3
Oxtail soup	½ pt (284 ml)	150	2
Pizza, cheese & tomato	1 small	260	6
Ploughman's lunch French bread & butter	4 oz (114 g) + 1 oz (30 g)	550	14
+ pâté	3 oz (85 g)	835	14
+ cheese only	3 oz (85 g)	710	14
+ cheese & sweet pickle	1 tbsp	750	16
Pork pie	1 average slice	630	9
Potato salad	8 oz (227 g)	250	8
Quiche lorraine	1 small slice	440	4
Ravioli	6 oz (171 g)	400	8
Roast beef	4 oz (114 g) +	400	—
+ yorkshire pudding	1 small	120	3
Sausages & beans	2 oz (57 g) + 5 oz (142 g)	400	5
Sausage, egg & bacon pie	6 oz (171 g)	550	5
Scotch broth	18 oz (511 g)	620	4
Scotch egg	1 large	550	4
Shepherd's pie	10 oz (284 g)	350	5

	Size of average portion	Calories per portion	Carbohydrate units per portion
Spanish omelette (2 eggs + vegetables)	8 oz (227 g)	290	1
Steak pie (individual)	8 oz (227 g)	750	11
Steak & kidney pudding	10 oz (284 g)	850	14
Stuffed pancakes			
meat filling	10 oz (284 g)	370	7
ham & mushrooms	10 oz (284 g)	410	7
Toasted sandwiches			
Bread	3 oz (85 g)		
Butter	$\frac{1}{2}$ oz (14 g)		
+ cheese	2 oz (57 g)	530	8
+ ham	$1\frac{1}{2}$ oz (43 g)	350	8
+ ham & cheese	1 oz (30 g) +		
	$1\frac{1}{2}$ oz (43 g)	450	8
Toad in the hole	6 oz (171 g)	480	5
Tripe & onions	7 oz (199 g)	170	2
Waldorf salad (celery, apples, nuts and mayonnaise)	4 oz (114 g)	130	2

PUDDINGS (Lunch)

Apple pie plain	6 oz (171 g)	300	8
+ custard	3 oz (85 g)	400	11
+ ice cream	2 oz (57 g)	395	11
+ whipped cream	1 tbsp	395	8

	Size of average portion	Calories per portion	Carbohydrate units per portion
Baked apples + sugar	6 oz (171 g)	60	4
+ butter & honey	6 oz (171 g)	120	5
+ dates & walnuts	6 oz (171 g)	125	5
+ mincemeat	6 oz (171 g)	115	5
+ dried fruits	6 oz (171 g)	125	6
Bakewell tart	4 oz (114 g)	480	10
+ custard	2 oz (57 ml)	550	12
Banana custard	6 oz (171 g)	180	6
Blancmange	6 oz (171 g)	200	7
Bread & butter pudding	8 oz (227 g)	460	12
Cheesecake lemon	4 oz (114 g)	430	5
+ currants	4 oz (114 g)	420	5
Fruit crumble (e.g. rhubarb)	8 oz (227 g)	440	14
Fruit jelly	5 oz (142 g)	115	6
Fruit fool (e.g. gooseberry)	8 oz (227 ml)	280	2
Fruit salad + sugar	6 oz (171 g)	160	7
Jam roly-poly	4 oz (114 g)	470	12
Lemon sponge pudding	4 oz (114 g)	440	10
Rice pudding	6 oz (171 g)	220	6
+ jam	2 tsp	260	8
Sherry trifle (sponge cake, fruit, custard, cream, sherry and nuts)	6 oz (171 g)	370	7
Treacle tart	3 oz (85 g)	320	10
+ custard	3 oz (85 g)	420	13

	Size of average portion	Calories per portion	Carbohydrate units per portion
DINNER (soups & starters)			
Artichokes + butter	4 oz (114 g)	50	—
Asparagus			
+ Hollandaise sauce	4 oz (114 g)	50	—
Avocado + prawn cocktail	4 oz (114 g)	270	$\frac{1}{2}$
Bortsch	$\frac{1}{2}$ pt (284 ml)	75	$\frac{1}{2}$
Chicken soup cream	$\frac{1}{2}$ pt (284 ml)	140	2
Chicken noodle soup	$\frac{1}{2}$ pt (284 ml)	55	2
Consommé	$\frac{1}{2}$ pt (284 ml)	70	—
Corn on the cob + butter	1 medium	280	6
Crab mousse	6 oz (171 g)	200	2
Cream of watercress soup	$\frac{1}{2}$ pt (284 ml)	150	2
Cucumber soup	$\frac{1}{2}$ pt (284 ml)	210	2
Duck pâté	2 oz (57 g)	190	3
+ toast & butter	2 slices	410	6
Egg mayonnaise	1 egg	180	—
Farmhouse pâté	4 oz (114 g)	300	—
French onion soup	$\frac{1}{2}$ pt (284 ml)	270	4
Garlic bread	2 oz (57 g)	220	5
Gazpacho	12 oz (341 g)	260	3
Grilled grapefruit + sugar	$\frac{1}{2}$ medium + 2 tsp	65	4
Ham mousse	6 oz (171 g)	125	$\frac{1}{2}$
Houmous	2 oz (57 g)	200	$\frac{1}{2}$
Kipper pâté	3 oz (85 g)	230	—

	Size of average portion	Calories per portion	Carbohydrate units per portion
Leeks Vinaigrette	4 oz (114 g)	170	—
Melon & Parma Ham	12 oz (341 g)	230	2
Moules marinières	10 oz (284 g)	310	—
Mulligatawny soup	½ pt (284 ml)	100	3
Mushrooms à la grècque	6 oz (171 g)	275	—
Mushroom soup cream	½ pt (284 ml)	150	2
Oysters	6 oz (171 g)	135	—
Piperade (+ croutons)	6 oz (171 g)	110	2
Potted shrimps	3 oz (85 g)	230	—
Ratatouille	10 oz (284 g)	170	—
Rollmops	2 rolls	280	—
Salmon mousse	6 oz (171 g)	380	2
Samosas	4 oz (114 g)	390	11
Savoury choux buns (with cheese)	3 oz (85 g)	270	2
Shellfish cocktail	3 oz (85 g)	200	—
Smoked salmon	2 oz (57 g)	80	—
Smoked trout	1 small	200	—
Stuffed tomatoes (cheese, ham, breadcrumbs)	1 large	160	2
Taramasalata	2 oz (57 g)	180	1
+ pitta bread	1 piece	400	11
Tuna & bean salad	7 oz (199 g)	320	4
Whitebait fried	3 oz (85 g)	450	1
Vol au vents + chicken & mushroom	10 oz (284 g)	570	6

	Size of average portion	Calories per portion	Carbohydrate units per portion
DINNER (main courses)			
Bean curd + prawns	5 oz (142 g)	330	1
Beef goulash	15 oz (426 g)	600	5
Beef stroganoff	15 oz (426 g)	580	1
Boeuf bourguignonne	20 oz (567 g)	570	2
Boeuf en croûte	5 oz (142 g)	360	3
Bouillabaisse	$\frac{1}{2}$ pt (284 ml)	450	2
Braised red cabbage	6 oz (171 g)	120	3
Carbonnade of beef	18 oz (511 g)	720	6
Cassoulet	16 oz (454 g)	650	6
Cheese soufflé	16 oz (454 g)	650	6
Cheese fondue	10 oz (284 g)	850	14
Chicken with almonds	8 oz (227 g)	860	1
Chicken chasseur	12 oz (341 g)	370	1
Chicken kiev	10 oz (284 g)	780	8
Chicken koorma	12 oz (341 g)	900	1
Chicken Maryland (with banana, cornfritter and bacon)	15 oz (426 g)	1050	15
Chicken pilau	10 oz (284 g)	480	10
Chilli con carne	12 oz (341 g)	440	4
Chop suey	10 oz (284 g)	270	1
Chow mein	13 oz (369 g)	660	20
Croque Monsieur	8 oz (227 g)	430	5
Crown roast of lamb	7 oz (199 g)	620	3
Dolmades	4 oz (114 g)	140	2

	Size of average portion	Calories per portion	Carbohydrate units per portion
Duckling à l'orange	18 oz (511 g)	800	5
Filet mignon	10 oz (284 g)	335	—
Fried scampi + tartare sauce	7 oz (199 g)	700	11
Fried sweetbreads	4 oz (114 g)	260	1
Game pie	12 oz (341 g)	920	12
Glazed baked gammon	7 oz (199 g)	400	3
Indonesian beef satay	6 oz (171 g)	520	—
Lamb biryani	16 oz (454 g)	670	15
Lamb kebabs	7 oz (199 g)	660	1
Lasagne verdi	12 oz (341 g)	900	10
Leeks & ham au gratin	12 oz (341 g)	430	5
Lobster thermidor	12 oz (341 g)	570	1
Macaroni cheese	10 oz (284 g)	500	10
Moussaka	10 oz (284 g)	550	5
Mushroom & ham risotto	10 oz (284 g)	230	10
Paella (including rice, veg., and seafoods)	20 oz (567 g)	630	13
Peppered steak + cream sauce	7 oz (199 g)	740	1
Pork chop casserole	12 oz (341 g)	660	2
Pork in cider	16 oz (454 g)	600	4
Prawn biryani + chutney	13 oz (369 g)	730	20
Sag gosht	12 oz (341 g)	460	1
Salmon & hollandaise sauce	6 oz (171 g)	490	—

	Size of average portion	Calories per portion	Carbohydrate units per portion
Saltimbocca	5 oz (142 g)	340	1
Sole véronique (with cream + grapes)	12 oz (341 g)	400	2
Spaghetti bolognese	15 oz (426 g)	550	15
Steak tartare	7 oz (199 g)	350	3
Stuffed baked potatoes			
+ cheese	1 large	430	9
+ bacon	1 large	250	9
+ smoked salmon	1 large	230	9
+ cream & chives	1 large	220	9
+ pickle & cottage cheese	1 large	240	10
Stuffed marrow	12 oz (341 g)	330	4
Stuffed peppers	14 oz (397 g)	390	8
Sweet & sour pork	8 oz (227 g)	720	7
Sweet & sour prawns in batter	10 oz (284 g)	530	10
Sukiyaki	13 oz (369 g)	350	3
Tandoori chicken	12 oz (341 g)	290	—
Trout with almonds	14 oz (397 g)	670	3
Welsh rarebit	4 oz (114 g)	420	5
Wiener schnitzel	6 oz (171 g)	360	2

PUDDINGS (dinner)

Baked Alaska (sponge cake, ice cream and meringue)	8 oz (227 g)	510	20
Banana flambée	5 oz (142 g)	400	10

	Size of average portion	Calories per portion	Carbohydrate units per portion
Caramel oranges	5 oz (142 g)	200	9
Charlotte russe	6 oz (171 g)	475	8
Chocolate mousse	4 oz (114 g)	320	5
Chocolate soufflé	6 oz (171 g)	350	9
Chocolate profiteroles	6 oz (171 g)	340	7
Christmas pudding	5 oz (142 g) +	410	14
+ brandy butter	1 oz (30 g)	550	16
Crème brûlée	6 oz (171 g)	700	6
Crème caramel	6 oz (171 g)	230	8
Crêpes suzette	6 oz (171 g)	475	9
Fresh fruit salad	6 oz (171 g)	85	5
Lemon meringue pie	4 oz (114 g)	370	10
Lemon sorbet	5 oz (142 g)	190	6
Pears in red wine	8 oz (227 g)	225	12
Queen of puddings	6 oz (171 g)	360	11
Rum baba	6 oz (171 g)	430	13
Strawberries	6 oz (171 g)	45	2
+ sugar	2 tsp	85	4
+ sugar & cream (double)	2 tsp + 1 oz (30 g)	210	4
Strawberry shortcake	5 oz (142 g)	420	9
Summer pudding	8 oz (227 g)	330	11
Syllabub	5 oz (142 g)	480	8
Zabaglione	2 oz (57 g)	190	8

Index